"*Don't Believe the Swipe* is another Mandy Hale essential read. So funny, so smart and cutting—I'm jealous I didn't write it."

Greg Behrendt, *New York Times* bestselling coauthor, *He's Just Not That Into You*

"Where has this book been all my life? Funny, wise, and oh so clever . . . it's seriously the last dating book I'll ever need."

Krista Allen, actress, comedian, recovering believer in the swipe

"As a fellow single, I am so happy to have this new book by Mandy Hale to help me think and laugh my way to finding the love of my life. Mandy has a way with words that blesses the journey, even on the tough days."

Yvette Nicole Brown, actress, comedian, writer, and TV host

"*Don't Believe the Swipe* is a hilarious and candid guide to navigating dating as a modern single woman. Mandy shares her tales from the swiping front lines, teaches you every pitfall to avoid, and, above all, inspires self-love and hopefulness for anyone still waiting to meet their perfect match."

Francesca Hogi, celebrity love and life coach

"This book cuts through the fog of modern dating and reconnects us to our single most important relationship—the relationship we have with ourselves."

Devyn Simone, celebrity matchmaker, dating expert, and TV host

"*Don't Believe the Swipe* is a primer on modern dating. This book made me cry and cringe and laugh and lament, and at the end of it, I feel less alone and better able to tackle this crazy dating world."

Joy Beth Smith, author, *Party of One*

Don't Believe the Swipe

Don't Believe the Swipe

Finding Love *without* Losing Yourself

Mandy Hale

Revell
a division of Baker Publishing Group
Grand Rapids, Michigan

Published by Revell
a division of Baker Publishing Group
PO Box 6287, Grand Rapids, MI 49516-6287
www.revellbooks.com

Printed in the United States of America

Library of Congress Cataloging-in-Publication Data
Names: Hale, Mandy, 1978– author.
Title: Don't believe the swipe : finding love without losing yourself / Mandy Hale.
Description: Grand Rapids, Michigan : Revell, a division of Baker Publishing Group, [2021]
Identifiers: LCCN 2020024619 | ISBN 9780800738839 (paperback)
Subjects: LCSH: Dating (Social customs) | Man-woman relationships. | Interpersonal relations.
Classification: LCC HQ801 .H3125 2021 | DDC 646.7/7—dc23
LC record available at https://lccn.loc.gov/2020024619

ISBN 978-0-8007-4034-4 (casebound)

The names and details of the people and situations described in this book have been changed or presented in composite form.

Published in association with The Bindery Agency, www.TheBinderyAgency.com.

21 22 23 24 25 26 27 7 6 5 4 3 2 1

For all the single girls
still brave enough to believe in love.

And for our frontline health-care heroes.
THANK YOU.

Contents

Modern Dating Dictionary

To understand modern dating, we must first understand the terminology. The list below, though not exhaustive, contains some of the most popular terms used to describe modern dating (though there will no doubt be new words invented between now and when this book goes to print). Some words I've heard from various sources, some I found online, and others I completely made up. (The terms I made up are denoted as "Mandy originals.") All definitions are translated into my own voice—because this is my book and I can do that.

bae: It's not as commonly used anymore . . . but the classics never really go out of style, so it's still worthy of inclusion. *Bae* is your significant other or someone you want to *be* your significant other.

benching: When someone puts one romantic prospect on ice in favor of another one they find more promising. They will continue to come around and drop just enough crumbs to keep you interested in case the other relationship doesn't work out, but there's no real investment or intention behind their sparse communication.

bird-boxing: Inspired by the wildly popular Netflix film, this is when someone refuses to see or acknowledge just how truly toxic their relationship is.

boo: Your significant other.

boo'd up: When you have a boo and are officially off the market.

breadcrumbing: When someone drops just enough breadcrumbs to keep you interested without actually engaging in a relationship or meaningful communication. That guy who texts you "WYD" every other Thursday night and on holidays? Total breadcrumber. *Breadcrumbing* is a modernized term for leading someone on.

Caspering: Friendly ghosting, aka when both parties clearly don't want to see each other again after the first or second date so they mutually vanish from each other's lives.

catching feelings: Developing feelings for someone.

catfishing: A term made popular by the hit MTV show of the same name. This is when someone essentially poses as someone else, even down to stealing their photos and life details, in order to attract people online.

cloaking (aka the new *ghosting*): Picture Harry Potter in his invisibility cloak. While being ghosted means your love interest has gone completely radio silent, cloaking takes it one step further. A cloaker doesn't just cease communication, they block you on dating apps, their phones, and social media. They essentially might as well be invisible because, to you, they no longer exist.

cuffing: When two people who have been dating each other for a while decide they want to date only each other. Taken from the term *handcuffs*, cuffing is when you choose to link hands *and* lives.

cuffing season: The time of year when people are most in the mood to commit and most likely to settle down, which tends to be September through February (i.e., the chilly months, the cozy months, the snuggling months, the holiday months). March through August (*"Summer, summer, summertime!"*) finds people scurrying out of hibernation and back on the prowl.

curving: A tactic deployed when you want to let someone down easy. Basically, the kinder, gentler rejection. Example: A guy you're not into texts to tell you how pretty you looked today when he ran into you at the coffee shop and casually drops a "We should hang out sometime." You respond with "Awww, you're so sweet!" thereby technically responding to his text in a nice way while curving the conversation away from the idea of actually hanging out.

deep-like: Contrary to what you might be thinking, no, this is not when you like someone a whole lot. A deep-like is when you're stalking your crush's Instagram feed and you accidentally like a pic from, say, five years ago . . . thereby completely outing yourself and your social media stalking ways. Sorry, friends—not even putting your phone on rice will get you out of this one.

dial-toning: When you give someone your digits, they reach out, and you never respond.

dogfishing: When guys post multiple pics with their dogs on dating apps to appear extra cute and cuddly to the opposite sex.

double-booker (Mandy original): A person who books more than one date in one day.

double-texting: When you text someone twice (or more times) in a row before they have responded to your first text.

exting (Mandy original): Texting your ex.

fleabagging: When you keep choosing to date guys who are the absolute worst for you, over and over and over and over and over and over and over again.

ghosting: Possibly the first and most well-known of the modern dating terms. Ghosting is when you are talking to or dating someone and they disappear into thin air, never to be heard from again. (Or possibly to be heard from again, if they zombie you.) Ghosting usually comes out of nowhere, with no apparent warning signs, and typically leaves the ghosted feeling completely hurt and baffled. Most ghosting tends to take place in the early stages of dating; however, some people have been known to ghost on long-term relationships. When this happens, there's not much the ghosted can do except pick up the pieces and move on.

glamboozled: When you're all decked out in your LBD (Little Black Dress) and ready for date night and your date bails on you at the last minute . . . via text.

haunted house: When you are at the same function as two or more people who ghosted you (*#awkward!*).

Houdini-ing: More of a gradual ghosting. This is when, instead of disappearing abruptly, the person you're dating slowly tapers off their communication until one day they just—*poof!*—disappear into thin air.

kittenfishing: When someone showcases photos of themselves that are all ten-plus years old on dating apps. Meaning they're kinda catfishing you . . . with the past version of them.

leave him/her on read: Phones have a setting that allows you to turn on read receipts so a sender can see when you've read their text. The reference *leave him on read* or *leave her on read* basically means you've read their text but didn't respond, either purposely or not purposely. But most of the time, as it is related to this reference, it's purposely. Usually, when you leave someone on read, it's to send the message that you're upset with them, you're over their nonsense, or you're just not that into them.

love bombing: When someone wines and dines and romances you so hard you feel like Cinderella at the ball meeting her dashing Prince Charming. A person who love bombs is a first-class future faker and, within a week, will be dropping the L-bomb and making plans to meet your parents. The problem? When the clock strikes midnight, the roses and candy and cute pet names and empty promises and declarations of love will all disappear faster than Cinderella's carriage turned into a pumpkin. Because you've been hit by . . . you've been struck by . . . a love bomber.

Michael Myers (Mandy original): Inspired by the villain who simply won't die in the *Halloween* movies. A Michael Myers is an ex who keeps popping up in your life, and you can't seem to get rid of him no matter what you do.

monkeying: When someone hops from relationship to relationship at breakneck speed. Also known as a serial dater.

mosted (Mandy original): When a man does the absolute most to come across as a good guy (sweet, innocent, maybe even a little nerdy) only to end up being a bad boy (player, cheater, ghoster). This is sort of a second cousin to the love bomber, except minus the grand romantic gestures.

Netflix and chill: When your love interest invites you over under the guise of a Netflix bingefest, but as the night goes on, you realize he's less interested in the latest season of *Outlander* and more interested in just making out.

nexting (Mandy original): When a guy is already texting or trolling online for the next girl to date before he's even ended things with his current girlfriend.

orbiting: This most infuriating phenomenon is when the person you're seeing, or have at least been out with a couple of times, either ends things or ghosts you but then continues to watch your Instagram stories, share your TikToks, scope your Snapchat, like your Facebook posts, and essentially stalk you across all social media platforms until the end of time. Why do they care to keep up with you online but not in real time? The world may never know.

pocketing: When someone you've been seeing for a decent amount of time still hasn't introduced you to their friends or family.

relationship reboot (Mandy original): When you attempt to resurrect an ex or recycle a relationship.

roaching: When the person you've been seriously or somewhat seriously dating—though maybe haven't yet had "the talk" with—conceals the fact that they've also been seeing other people. When you learn about their roach-like habits and confront them, they feign innocence and claim they had no clue that the two of you were in an exclusive relationship.

seek*her* (Mandy original): Derived from the word *seeker*, a seek*her* is a man who monkeys his way through relationship after relationship at lightning pace, ever seeking but never finding. He's only comfortable *looking* for love and not actually finding it, because if he found it, he would actually have to commit to someone. This species of man *says* he wants to find his dream woman, but the truth is, he'd much prefer the safety of continuing to seek her for the rest of his life over the danger of actually finding her.

side chick: When a man you're dating has a more serious romantic connection, or even a full-blown relationship, with someone else and you are his number-two draft pick . . . the unfortunate term for you in this equation would be the *side chick*. Most of the time side chicks are unwittingly side chicks, but some women are sadly and knowingly content to play second fiddle to another woman as long as they get to be in the band.

situationship: A romantic situation that is more than a friendship but less than a relationship. Basically, the gray area or purgatory of modern dating. Some people linger in situationships for *years*, waiting and hoping to hit the tipping point into Love Town, but unfortunately, most situationships never leave the city limits of Ambiguous, population 2.

sliding into the DMs: When you have a crush on someone on a social media platform and you make your move by sending them a direct message (aka DM).

textationship: One level down from a situationship, a textationship is when you have a "relationship" with someone that consists only of texting, never hanging out in person and possibly never even meeting face-to-face at all. You'd be surprised (or, actually, you probably wouldn't) at how many men seem perfectly content to never advance beyond a textationship.

thirst trap: When you post an overtly sexy photo or flirty message on social media strictly for the purpose of getting someone's attention. Thirst traps are called thirst traps because they come across as somewhat desperate and "thirsty." If you want to post a bomb photo of yourself, post it for you, not to get a response from the person who's been ignoring you for the past month.

unsolved mystery (Mandy original): Coined in reference to the super creepy 1980s show hosted by Robert Stack and, of course, the current Netflix bingeworthy rage. This is when someone ghosts you in a particularly baffling manner and you never get an explanation of any kind. With a regular ghosting, often you'll see pics online of the person who ghosted you with their ex or their new significant other and it will become clear *why* they ghosted you. With an unsolved mystery, you never get an explanation or clarity of any kind. It's a ghosting that haunts you, in other words.

zombie-ing: When someone ghosts you, then reanimates long enough to come back into your life, act interested, and get you back on the hook, only to then turn right around and ghost you again.

Prologue

It was New Year's Eve. I had been seeing an ex of mine again (mistake number one), as I was making a second attempt at fashioning a relationship out of a situationship (see "Modern Dating Dictionary"). The ex—let's call him Chandler Bing—and I had plans for that evening, which was a really big deal for me, as I hadn't had a New Year's Eve date since *Friends* was still on the air. I was nervous and excited and completely atwitter about the thought of a New Year's Eve kiss. I had gone shopping earlier that week for the perfect outfit, and my hair, nails, and eyebrows were on fleek, as the kids say. (Do the kids still say that?) I was ready for a night to remember!

Chandler Bing and I didn't have a set plan, and being a type-A control freak, I don't do well when there isn't a set plan . . . so, around noon I shot him a text: "What's the plan for tonight?" Within short order, a meandering response came through that said something to the effect of "Well, right now I'm at home in bed, sick. I think I'm going to head to the walk-in clinic in a bit and see what they say, and then I can let you know something."

My heart dropped. I'm sure every woman reading this right now can read between the lines of that text. What he *was* saying seemed simple enough: he was "sick." What he *wasn't* saying? He was most likely going to bail on our big New Year's Eve plans. The minute a guy—or really anyone, for that matter—plants the first seemingly innocuous seed that there *might* possibly be a reason they won't be able to make plans, you can pretty much expect that seed to blossom into a full-bloom tree of cancellation. It's just the way of the modern world. Technology, texting, and social media have made it possible to avoid all awkwardness by never having to see people face-to-face (only Facebook-to-Facebook) to cancel plans. Since Chandler Bing was notoriously flaky anyway, I had a sinking feeling that, come midnight, the only kiss I would be experiencing would be of the Hershey's persuasion.

I texted back something light and breezy like, "Okay, keep me posted!" But I was most definitely not feeling breezy. I was feeling the exact opposite of breezy. I was feeling like heavy cloud cover with a 100 percent chance of rain. And throw in a tornado watch for good measure. Chandler Bing had bailed on me before, using a similar excuse to the one he had just delivered to my inbox. Would he really bail on me on New Year's Eve?! My female intuition was telling me yes.

I needed to find out exactly what I was dealing with. I needed to deploy . . . the drive-by.

What is the drive-by, you might be wondering? Well, if you're a woman who has spent five minutes in the dating world, you won't need an explanation; however, I am going to pretend for a moment that aliens who are visiting Planet Earth for the first time picked up my book and have no idea what I'm talking about. The drive-by is pretty much exactly what it sounds like: a casual drive by the house of the guy you're dating to see if he is indeed at home like he claims to be, or if he's not and you are being hoodwinked. It must be carried out carefully and covertly, so as not to get caught (because you don't want him thinking you're Love Quinn from *You* on Netflix).

The problem with Chandler Bing's house was that it was nearly impossible to drive by and see if his car was there without getting busted. His driveway was surrounded by a fence, so you could only see whether or not his car was there if you drove around to the back and down a narrow alley. A narrow alley that was about four feet away from his back door. A narrow alley that you would then have to turn around in and drive back down in order to exit. If he was home and he happened to walk outside or even just glance outside as you were driving by . . . there was zero chance of not getting caught.

I want to interject here that I don't make a habit of the drive-by. It truly is a last resort. But this was New Year's Eve, folks. It was noon on New Year's Eve, and my date was being flakier than a bowl of Frosted Flakes. It was officially time to ring the alarm. I needed answers.

So that's how, on New Year's Eve, I found myself ordering a Lyft to come and pick me up and drive me by Chandler Bing's house. Because, you know, nothing says "inconspicuous" like a car with a giant pink mustache on the front.

I'm not proud of my decision. I cringe at the thought that there was a time not so long ago when I allowed the swipe to so dramatically control my life. "The swipe" being the endless search for a man's approval, attention, validation, affection, etc.—a phenomenon created by the weird and random mating ritual of dating apps, where we wait with bated breath for someone to "swipe right" on us, indicating they might want to spend the rest of their life with us based on a brief bio and a handful of photos. And it pains me to admit I believed, in that moment, that what the swipe seemed to be saying about me was more important than what *I* knew about me. But I can also look back and find the humor in the situation as I picture myself in my pajamas, diving down in the backseat of a random Lyft driver's car as she sped me past my ex's house to see if he really was home sick or if he was being shadier than a pool umbrella.

My driver was a woman, so of course she immediately *got it.* But that didn't stop her from cackling as I swaddled myself in a blanket, ET-style, and hunkered down in the backseat, yelling directions to Chandler Bing's house from the floorboard so as not to be spotted.

He wasn't home (no big surprise there), so I asked my driver to cruise past the walk-in clinic near his house, and what do you know? He wasn't there either. It appeared that Chandler Bing had in fact fibbed about his illness, which meant he was most likely setting me up for a New Year's Eve no-show.

I know some of you are probably thinking, *Overreacting much? Maybe he was at the store getting some DayQuil and Kleenex and chicken soup. Perhaps there's a perfectly reasonable explanation for his claiming to be sick in bed and yet actually not being at home when you drove by his house.* And I get it. I, too, always want to give people the benefit of the doubt. But with Chandler Bing . . . the shady, flaky, slippery explanation was almost always the right one. And by that point I had already dated him once and watched our relationship blow up in my face due to his dishonesty. So, while it was unfortunate that he was being less than honest with me again and was likely going to disappoint me again . . . it wasn't at all surprising.

But. That's not even the main point I'm trying to make with this story.

The point I want to make with this humiliating yet also painfully hilarious story is this:

If you find yourself hunched down in the backseat of a Lyft driver's car on New Year's Eve, lightly stalking your ex-boyfriend to see if he's lying to you again . . . something has clearly gone wrong. And you're letting the swipe rule your life.

If you find yourself compromising your dignity or self-respect in any way to find a man, get a man, or keep a man . . . you're letting the swipe rule your life.

If you find yourself moonlighting as a private detective, trying to figure out what he's doing, thinking, saying, intending, feeling, or not feeling . . . you're letting the swipe rule your life.

If dating feels less like fun and more like torture . . . you're letting the swipe rule your life.

If you are allowing any other human being or their behavior to define the way you feel about yourself . . . you're letting the swipe rule your life.

If being with him, seeing him, talking to him, texting him, casually dating him, seriously dating him, underwater basket weaving with him . . . is in *any* way causing you to sacrifice your peace of mind, your confidence, your happiness, your family, your friends, your finances, your self-worth, your self-esteem, or yourself . . . you're letting the swipe rule your life.

If you are hinging your sense of wholeness and well-being on something as arbitrary and random and inconsequential as a dating app . . . you're letting the swipe rule your life.

And if you are in fact letting the swipe rule your life . . . this book is designed to help you stop the madness, reclaim yourself, and start swiping right on *yourself*. Because what good is it to find love if you lose yourself in the process?

I am happy to tell you, that fateful New Year's Eve, crouching in the backseat of a Lyft driver's car, was the last time I gave my power away to any man or anyone or anything. And it was also the last time I let the swipe rule my life.

That experience helped shake me awake and open my eyes to just how much I was allowing dating apps and Chandler Bing and, really, every guy I dated to control how I felt about *me*. And in the two years since that happened, I've shifted the focus to myself and to *my* growth: mentally, physically, emotionally, and spiritually. I've recommitted to therapy. I've confronted my own junk. I've taken dating hiatuses when I needed a break. I've done the hard work on myself so that now I can look for love and hope for love and pray for love and wish for love while also being grounded in the knowledge that if I never find it, or if it never finds me . . . I'll be okay.

And so will you.

Did you know that almost every modern dating book that has been lauded as groundbreaking has been written by a man? It's true. They always tend to be framed from the male perspective: What a man wants. How to act like a man. Get any man to fall in love with you. The list goes on and on. How completely nonsensical is that? I mean, I don't know about you . . . but I don't exactly see a ton of men frequenting the "Dating and Romance" aisle at the bookstore. Women are the ones reading the books, so shouldn't women be the ones writing them? That's why I knew it was time to take matters into my own hands and write a definitive book about the modern dating experience from the female perspective. To put the power *back* in the hands of women instead of making it all about the man. Why am I qualified to write this book, you might ask? Well, I have twenty-five years of dating experience. I've dated some good guys and some total doofuses (I have to interject here that *doofi* is also the plural of *doofus* and that just slays me). I've used dating apps, and I've met guys organically. I've been the dumper and the dump-ee. I've taken months-long (and even years-long!) hiatuses from dating. I have a ton of single girlfriends who share their fairy-tale stories and their horror stories with me. I have a gold mine of amazing male friends whom I'm able to tap for advice, encouragement, and answers to my most burning questions about the male species. I have three-million-plus social media followers who confide in me their most heartwarming and heart-stopping dating tales on a daily basis. And I'm out here with all of you in this modern dating world, a new frontier that is vastly different from the dating world of even five years ago. I'm not writing to you from a pedestal of happily ever after; I am down here with you in the trenches of *The Hunger Games* that is modern dating. It is not for the faint of heart. And since it doesn't come with a guidebook, I thought . . . why not write one?

We're going to cover it all in this book, or at least all the factors that I think most contribute to the mystery of modern dating:

Online dating/dating apps. First dates. Bad dates. Ghosting. Texting. Exting. Breakups. Makeups. Zombie-ing. Kittenfishing. Monkeying. (Yes, these are all actual modern dating phenomenon and precisely why this book features a Modern Dating Dictionary.) We're also going to answer some age-old burning questions: Can men and women really be friends? Are men really ever "intimidated" by women, or is that an excuse they use when they're just not that into us? Were Ross and Rachel *really* on a break? (Okay, we're not going to answer that one. That one will forever remain a mystery.) And, most of all, we're going to learn how to *stop* believing the swipe . . . and how to find love without losing ourselves. Because, at the end of the day, whether or not someone chooses you means absolutely nothing if you don't choose yourself.

Before we begin, however, I want to share with you how my New Year's Eve story turned out, because it has a surprise ending. Although Chandler Bing *did* lie to me about being home sick, he *didn't* actually end up canceling our New Year's Eve plans! (*What?!*) And I did get my New Year's Eve kiss, though it was a little delayed. To ring in the New Year, we drove to the top of a renowned lookout point in my small town, which offers a breathtaking view of the lights below. And as the clock struck twelve, we clinked our sparkling cider glasses together and drew closer and closer, until . . .

A cop came banging on our window and told us to leave (cue the crying-laughing emoji).

Yep, he mistook us for high school kids who were parking and ordered us right off our romantic perch. Ha! Kinda gives new meaning to the phrase "Stop in the name of love."

Okay, friends . . . picture me now as that cop, banging on the window of your lives and stopping you in your dating tracks. It's time to *stop in the name of love* and realize that singleness and even dating don't have to be about landing a man or chasing a man or getting a man to choose you, validate you, or fall in love with you. They can and should be about falling in love with *yourself* and extending that love to every aspect of your life, surrendering control to the process without surrendering your personal power, and choosing yourself, regardless of whether anyone swipes right or swipes left.

There *is* a way to date with dignity, to refuse to let the swipe rule your life, to stand confident in your worth and not settle for less than you deserve, and to find love without losing yourself. This book is that way.

Let's get started.

P.S. At the end of every chapter, you'll find a "Rule to Re-*meme*-ber," which will feature a brief and highly meme-able footnote to the chapter . . . sort of a cherry on top of the sundae, if you will. These rules are purposely broken down into small sound bites to allow you to share them across your social media platforms. That way, when someone sees you strutting your newly empowered stuff and asks, "What's all the hype?" you can simply smile, give them a hair toss, and say, "Don't believe the swipe."

1

Modern Dating 101

Catch and Release

Once upon a time, in a land not so far away, a single woman and a single man both swiped right on each other and their story began.

They went out for pizza on their first date and ended up talking for four hours. Before they parted ways that night, he lined up their second date for a few days later.

On their second date, following a romantic dinner and a long moonlit stroll around a beautiful little town square, they sat on a park bench and talked for five hours. He gave her the best kind of butterflies, and when they parted ways that night, they sealed their date with a kiss—her first kiss in many months. He made it clear he wanted to see her again soon.

She drove home on cloud nine, her lips still warm from their perfect first kiss, already counting the days 'til they'd see each other again.

But somewhere between that night's farewell and the next morning's hello text . . . something shifted. His communication became sporadic, distant, and her gut started to twinge. Something was wrong.

Although she had only known him for a week or so, she had felt the "click" with him. That elusive click that only comes along every once in a while . . . when you just instantly and effortlessly mesh with someone and can start to see the first glimmers of something *real*.

Slowly, over the course of a few days, he tapered off his communication until it stopped altogether. He effectively Houdinied her. Their story was over before it had even begun. And she was crushed.

A few weeks later, he sent her a text apologizing for vanishing from her life but providing no real explanation as to why he did. To this day, what happened to so abruptly and drastically cause his feelings to change remains an unsolved mystery.

This, ladies and gentlemen, is a perfect snapshot of the mystery of modern dating. (By the way, in case you haven't figured it out yet—the girl in the story was me.)

Oh, the agony and defeat of modern dating.

(Before you get so depressed that you close this book and hurl it across the room, let me assure you that I'm giving you the bad news first. There is good news coming. I promise. So, make like the cat dangling from the tree in that popular vintage poster and hang in there.)

Why has dating become so difficult, so frustrating, so endlessly baffling? How did we get here? And how do we make it stop?

Well, first of all, modern dating feels about as appealing as reheating fast-food French fries for one very obvious reason: we've turned it into a fast-food experience. What do I mean by that? There are about a *million* different dating apps designed to foster love connections: Match, Bumble, Hinge, Facebook Dating, Tawkify, Coffee Meets Bagel, eHarmony, Christian Mingle, It's Just Lunch, Plenty of Fish, OkCupid, Raya, Tinder, The League . . . just to name a few. And most people are on at least two or three of these apps at any given time; meaning at any given time, they might be chatting with a dozen people (or more). When you have a seemingly endless array of options at your fingertips, just sitting and waiting for you to swipe right or left, it becomes impossible to go all the way in with one person because you're too busy going halfway in or a fourth of the way in with five or six people. It can feel both incredibly exhilarating and incredibly defeating to attempt to juggle five or six romantic connections at a time. (I can say this with confidence as someone who has double-booked before or—as defined in our Modern Dating Dictionary—been on two dates in one day.) Oh, and if it doesn't work out with one person? No prob! Just swipe on to the next! As quickly as you can zip through a drive-through line, you can swipe your way into a brand-new relationship, mere moments after the last one ended.

Ironically, it seems the *more* platforms modern technology gives us to help connect with one another, the *less* connected we actually are.

So, what's the fix? To swear off dating apps?

Absolutely not.

Because here's the good news (I told you it was coming): dating apps *can* work. I know they can work because I've had three relationships that were spawned from a dating app. I know people who are married as a result of swiping right. One of my friends and her fiancé were each other's first online dating connection, and a few years later, they're ready to walk down the aisle—all because they took a chance online. Another girlfriend of mine who met her husband online was on five dating apps at once and went out on twenty-nine first dates the year she met her future hubs. *Twenty-nine first dates!* I guess that proves that dating can in fact be a numbers game. It also proves that my friend is like the Leonardo DiCaprio of dating: just because she didn't win her Oscar (i.e., husband) on the first try didn't mean she was going to throw in the towel. And eventually, like Leo, she won!

So how can we do it? How can we still hope to become a wife without letting the swipe rule our life?

The art of catch and release, my friends.

The best piece of dating advice one of my best guy friends ever gave me was "Mandy, you must master the art of catch and release. You can't get so hung up on one guy who ghosts or Houdinis you that you miss out on the really great guy who might be coming along right after him."

With modern dating, you have to keep palms up, expectations down. Allow romantic prospects to flow in, and allow them to flow right back out.

Does this mean you should juggle more potential suitors at a time than Bozo the Clown or run through men faster than Blanche Devereaux? (If you don't know this reference, run to Hulu immediately and binge *The Golden Girls*, and don't come back to finish this book until you're done.) Not at all! But if you want a five-star reality, you have to ditch the fast-food mentality. Take your time getting to know one or even two connections at a time. It's not a race, nor should you collect men like Carrie Bradshaw collected shoes. It's not healthy, satisfying, or productive to have more boos than Casper the Friendly Ghost. And once a prospect makes it clear that they're not interested or that they're moving on . . . you must move on too. Catch and release. Leave the door of your heart open for Mr. Right to come in, and leave it open just as wide for Mr. Wrong to file back out. Don't cling, don't force, don't push, and don't try to stop people from leaving when they're ready to go.

The right one will come, and stay, without being asked, chased, or begged. You will never have to let go of your dignity and self-respect in order to hold on to the right love. Only the wrong love will require that.

Catch and release. Catch and release.

If you're venturing onto a dating app for the first time, here are a few more helpful hints:

1. While online dating and dating apps don't carry the same stigma they once did, figuring out which platform is best

for you can still feel a bit scary and overwhelming. While I don't have one app or platform to recommend over another, I will say it's important to do your research. Read online reviews, ask your single friends for their opinions, and hop on some of the apps to explore them for yourself. If one doesn't feel like a good fit, move on to the next one . . . just like you would with dating. (Catch and release.) Don't get discouraged if it takes some time to find your rhythm and start connecting with people. It took me a month to start making quality matches online, and sometimes it can take even longer. The best thing you can do is have fun and don't take it too seriously. Don't believe the swipe! Your happiness and your worth are not dependent on how many people you match with.

2. The bio: You have a few short sentences to tell the world who you are. Make them count. It's important to provide people with a glimpse into who you are and your personality rather than simply listing your stats like on the back of a baseball card. Humor is always good. I recommend staying away from anything too heavy or serious (e.g., "I haven't dated in two years because I've been mourning my divorce"); if you match and connect with someone, there's always time to get into serious stuff later. (But you have to match with them first, and maudlin and morose don't tend to inspire matchmaking.) Also, steer clear of any references to your ex. I've seen some men include a sentence in their bio about how they're "looking for someone who's not crazy like my ex," and I don't care if it's Jason Momoa himself . . . nothing makes me swipe left faster.
3. Pictures: Stay away from all heavily filtered and/or professional photos. Obviously, you want to put your best foot forward, but if every photo is a glamour shot, you're not giving people the chance to see the real you. It's good

to mix and match close-ups with full-body shots and also to include pics of you doing things you love to do. If you have six mirror-selfies, you're not offering a glimpse into who you are. I've had guy friends tell me they steer clear of profiles of women with all mirror-selfies because they come off as boring and lacking imagination. Ease off the Snapchat filters! I love a good filter as much as the next person, but make sure at least half of your photos are unfiltered and show you in your most honest light. Be sure to post recent photos, not ones from ten years ago. (You are far too fabulous to kittenfish!) You never want to show up to meet someone for dinner and have them not recognize you because you look so different from your photos.

4. Be yourself! Both on dating apps and when you start going out on dates. Don't be afraid to be very clear about what you're looking for or to keep it moving if you match with someone who doesn't fit the bill. Make sure your online dating profile showcases your personality and your *real* life, not some superperfect airbrushed version. Don't present yourself as a "lover of all things outdoors" if you've only been hiking once in your life. Remember, eventually you will meet some of these men in person and they'll be looking to meet the woman you presented yourself to be. So just be honest . . . be funny . . . be quirky . . . be creative . . . be authentic . . . but most of all, be YOU!
5. Online dating can make the process of meeting someone easier, but be sure to stay open to meeting people organically too. It can still happen! The chances of the perfect man being dropped on your doorstep are slim to none. (Although I *did* once date my upstairs neighbor—but I don't recommend that, because as it turns out, bumping

into your ex while taking out the trash sporting zit cream, rollers, and a onesie? Not tons of fun.) So you're going to have to put yourself out there and step out of your comfort zone a little. Join a new gym. Take up a new hobby. Join a meet-up group or find a new church or volunteer for a cause you're passionate about. The best, most organic way to meet someone who loves the things you love is by being active and getting out there and *doing* the things you love.

Overall, let your personality shine through your profile. There is a limited amount of space in which you can tell people you might want to date who you are. Put out there what you hope to attract in return. If you want to attract someone who's into the outdoors or plays or books or movies, make sure your profile reflects those interests. And above all . . . I can't state it enough times . . . be yourself. When you meet up with your connections in person, you want the person they meet to be as close as possible to the one in the profile they swiped right on.

Once you've got your colorful, fun, authentic profile up and going . . . the next big step is sending that first message to the men you connect with. And that can be intimidating, particularly if you're like me and prefer the guy to initiate. Here's where all the antiquated advice we've heard from books like *The Rules* starts to kick in. We resist moving with the times and realizing that it's a new day and that things have changed. And they have in fact changed. Whether we choose to adapt or to let our dating life suffer because of years of bad advice we've been given is up to us.

You want that first message to be cute and fun and something that stands out rather than just a generic "Hi." Most men on dating apps are likely getting hit with multiple messages from numerous women at any given time, and you don't want yours to get lost in the shuffle. My way of navigating this process so far has been to try to connect my first message back to something fun on his profile. (To that end, men on dating apps, *start filling out your bios*!) Even if his bio is blank, you can usually still find something in his profile pics that's conversation-worthy. And if not, you might just have to use your imagination and come up with something cute and flirty that's not related to his profile. As long as you stay away from the boring, unoriginal "Hi," you're golden. Now, all that said, you might have to warm up a bit and try a few different approaches before you find one that works. When I first started swiping, some of my opening lines were horribly cheesy. Interestingly enough, one of the corniest lines I ever used led to a month-long dating situation . . . so, I guess there's something to be said for cheesy.

The best way to approach online dating, or dating in general, is with an open hand. My therapist always likes to remind me not to "crush the butterfly." A butterfly is much prettier and more likely to hang around if you just allow it to land gently on your hand rather than grabbing, clutching, or squeezing it. The same can be said about relationships. It's all about the catch and release. Let whoever comes, come; and let whoever wants to go, go. Either way, you'll be okay. The wrong ones will go. The right ones will stay.

For the sake of clarity, before we move on let's quickly touch on the typical stages of modern dating.

If you meet online:

swiping
matching
chatting on the app
transition to texting
talking on the phone if you're both phone people (often this doesn't happen before the first date)
first date
second date

- if you're still communicating regularly after the second date, you're officially "talking"
- third date and beyond—you're dating, though nonexclusively
- "Let's be exclusive" talk
- boo'd up

If you meet organically:

- meeting
- exchanging phone numbers
- texting
- talking on the phone if you're both phone people (often this doesn't happen before the first date)
- first date
- second date
- if you're still communicating regularly after the second date, you're officially "talking"
- third date and beyond—you're dating, though nonexclusively
- "Let's be exclusive" talk
- boo'd up

RULE TO Re-meme-ber

Modern dating is rife with rejection. Every time I'm on a dating app, I get ghosted at least once a week. But luckily, I've done the hard work on myself and I am able to recognize that the way someone chooses to behave (in dating or in life) usually has nothing whatsoever to do with me. And it has nothing to do with you either. When someone doesn't choose you, don't internalize it; just let them go, and make room for the one who will! Catch and release, catch and release. Rest assured that if they ghost you, lie to you, cheat on you, break up with you, walk away from you, or act shady in any other way . . . THEY ARE NOT FOR YOU. Send them love and light, and then send them on their way. Don't waste time and energy trying to figure them out or trying to make sense of their shadiness or lack of character. It's water under the bridge. Don't believe the swipe, and move on with your life. Better things are coming.

Rest assured that if they ghost you, lie to you, cheat on you, break up with you, walk away from you, or act shady in any other way . . . THEY ARE NOT FOR YOU.

2

Dating Smarter, Not Harder

He Might Not Be Just Your Average Joe (Goldberg)

One of the most popular shows in the land of streaming right now is *You* on Netflix, starring Penn Badgley as cute-yet-obsessive-and-stalkerish Joe Goldberg. (I think only Penn Badgley could pull off cute and obsessively stalkerish at the same time.) While the show is creepily good and highly addictive, and although you might strangely find yourself cheering for Joe by the end of each season . . . there ain't nothing cute about being stalked. That's why it's so important, especially in the early stages of getting to know someone, not to get so carried away with following your heart that you forget to date smart.

Let's be all-the-way real: modern dating can be more than a little overwhelming at times. As someone who stepped back into the dating scene in my late thirties after a long hiatus, it took me a minute to adjust. Even before my dating break, I was never a regular dater. I've had only a handful of dating relationships in the past decade. So, it's safe to say . . . a lot changed during my time away. People text now instead of call. It's likely you won't even hear a guy's voice until you have your first date. The days of talking on the phone 'til the wee hours of the morning and learning everything there is to know about one another before you ever meet face-to-face seem to be a thing of the past. So how can you safely navigate dating apps, online dating, and meeting up with virtual strangers and ensure—as one of my lifelong friends would say—that you don't end up on an episode of *Dateline*? (Ha!)

One of the things I like about several current popular dating apps is that you set up your profile through your Facebook page, which makes it a lot harder for someone to fake their identity or to catfish you. A few of the apps will even show you if you have mutual Facebook friends, which gives you some sense of security, knowing that although the person you matched with might be a stranger, there are people you know who can vouch for him. All that said, you should still date with your head.

Wayyyyyy back on my very first meet-up with a guy from the first dating app I ever tried, I was still new and green to the whole thing, so I didn't have any rules or boundaries in place. (It's so important to establish some safety guidelines that you follow every single time you meet up with someone new.) I agreed to meet this guy at a restaurant without ever talking to him on the phone or asking for his last name. Truth be told, I felt a little awkward asking too many personal questions because I didn't want to come across as too untrusting or stalkerish. (Side note: It is not stalkerish to ask for a person's last name before you meet up with them. I was being silly and letting the swipe rule my life.) Anyway, over dinner, I did finally ask his last name, and that's when things got a little weird. Actually, things got a lot weird. It was like he was playing games or something—being coy—and for whatever reason, he refused to tell me his last name. He just kept saying, "If you really want to find out, you will." Here's where I will interject a note to the gentlemen: Guys, a first date with a girl who doesn't know you from Adam is *not* the time to play cute little coy games and refuse to give her even the most basic information about yourself. It *is* the time to put her mind at ease so she knows you're not hiding anything. That's not to say you should have to hand over your social security number or credit score, but, dang it, tell her your last name. Especially if you hope to have any chance of seeing her again. (Unless your goal is to make her think you're a serial killer. Or a Joe Goldberg. And remember, we already established that only Penn Badgley can pull off Joe Goldberg.)

That said, even though No Last Name Guy never did tell me his last name, he *did* pass along a very helpful safety tip: apparently when you enter someone's phone number into the search bar on Facebook, it pulls up their profile—or at least it does if they included their number in their profile. So, I was able to later learn the true identity of No Last Name Guy, and as it turns out, he wasn't a serial killer. Still, his evasiveness was off-putting, and that was, not surprisingly, our first and last date. But I walked away with a new resolve to establish some rules for myself to follow moving forward with first dates:

1. Always ask for the guy's last name prior to meeting up with him. The only way it will make you "come across" to him is smart and safe. And if he acts weird or put out by you asking him the most basic of questions, cancel the date and move on. He is not the one for you.
2. Try to have at least one phone conversation before meeting in person. Given the fast-paced, technology-driven, text-happy world we live in, this might not be possible. But it definitely helps establish a sense of safety and security to chat with someone and hear their voice and get to know the basics about them before that first face-to-face meeting. At the very least, communicate with him via

text to the extent that you feel like you've established a rapport. You never want to walk into a date with someone without any prior communication at all. That's uncomfortable and awkward for everyone.

3. Don't be shy about doing a little online vetting. Once I know a man's last name, I always scope out his Facebook or Instagram page. In this day and age, if a guy has no digital footprint whatsoever, that should be considered a red flag. Even if he's not social media savvy, he should still have a LinkedIn page or be searchable on Google. (Just make sure you don't accidentally deep-like his Instagram photo from two and a half years ago of him hula-hooping with his grandma in Hawaii or he'll think *you're* the Joe Goldberg.)
4. Always meet in a well-lit public place. I like to keep my first dates simple, like meeting for coffee or ice cream. Don't agree to go to a guy's house or have him over to yours for the first date. It's just not worth the risk. The added bonus of keeping the first date low-key is if you're having a terrible time, you can always ease on down the road in an hour or less. Whereas if you plan dinner and a movie, you could be stuck for three or four hours.
5. Finally, tell a friend or family member where you'll be and who you'll be with. Having someone aware of your whereabouts is Safety 101. Once, I agreed to go to the Opryland Hotel in Nashville to see their famous Christmas light display and have dinner with a guy I met the prior weekend. That meant a forty-five-minute drive there, at least two to three hours at the hotel, and a forty-five-minute drive back together. Normally I would never be down for such a marathon first date, but I'm a sucker for Christmas and for the absolutely breathtaking Opryland Hotel. Even though I knew the guy's last name

> and had checked him out online, I was still a bit nervous to travel any real distance with a guy I had just met and knew very little about. So I used the location-sharing feature on my phone and shared my location with my mom for the evening, and she was able to track my whereabouts at all times. This may sound a bit extreme, but I don't think you can be too cautious when it comes to your safety.

I love that old adage that says, "Follow your heart but take your brain with you." Short, sweet, simple . . . and true. I've luckily never found myself in a situation where I genuinely didn't feel safe, but it's always better to *be* safe than sorry. And any man who is worth your affections is going to understand and respect your taking basic safety precautions. Dating and dating apps can and should be fun. But as with anything else in life, you need to establish some healthy boundaries. That way you're free to risk your heart without compromising your safety.

RULE TO Re-meme-ber

SET BOUNDARIES, with your heart, your time, your dating life. Not everyone who knocks on the door of your life should be allowed in. Boundaries have the beautiful effect of weeding out people who don't belong there. People who truly want to be in your life and are meant to be in your life will *always* be willing to honor your boundaries and meet you halfway (or at least tell you their last name!) . . . and if they're not willing to meet you halfway, perhaps they shouldn't be given the pleasure of meeting you at all. Cultivate discernment, take your time, ask the questions you need to ask, and get to know people; and only then welcome them into your life. Trust is to be earned, not just handed out freely.

SET BOUNDARIES, with your heart, your time, your dating life. Not everyone who knocks on the door of your life should be allowed in.

3

Men Are from Netflix, Women Are from Hulu

The Great Communication Breakdown

We have more ways than ever to communicate with members of the opposite sex. A man has countless ways to convey the message that you are the one he wants to Netflix and chill with. He can text, he can (gasp!) call, or, if he's not brave enough for phone-on-phone action, he can slide into your DMs on any number of social platforms. I don't know if it's modern-day communication or modern-day men in general that cause us the greatest amounts of heartburn, but the three biggest issues I see single ladies struggling with stem from a total communication breakdown. Despite all the methods of communication we have available to us, we're not actually, well, communicating. There seems to be a Grand Canyon–sized chasm between the expectations women have and the expectations men are willing to meet when it comes to the art of communication.

So, what are the three communication gaps in dating that are trending right now and seem to be driving single women the most bonkers? Glad you asked.

1. No follow-through. He shows interest. He flirts. He bee-lines to your side the minute he sees you out somewhere. The message is clear. He's into you! So when he *finally* asks for your number, you think it's just a matter of time before he calls, you go out, you fall in love, you live happily ever after. Right? Wrong! Instead, he texts you half-heartedly a couple of times before dropping off the radar completely. (In other words, a total Houdini.)

   So, what gives? Why do these mysterious creatures known as the male species ask for a girl's number and act interested if they actually have no intention of following through? I hear phrases tossed around a lot like, "He's shy" and "He's intimidated" (we're going to talk more about this later) and "He's too busy right now," but in my experience, a man who sees something he *really* wants tends to go after it.
2. Infrequent communication. This is an offshoot of number one; however, this applies more to men who don't drop off completely but instead vanish for weeks at a time only to pop up randomly with a phone call or a drive-by "Hey, pretty lady!" text. (In other words, a total bread-crumber.) What is the point of this nonsense? When you talk, things seem great. You laugh, you vibe, you have a grand old time. So why doesn't he come around more often? This puzzles me more than the finale of *Game of Thrones*.
3. Banishing himself to the Island of Misfit Boys. (In other words, a total ghoster.) You're finally dating. You've worked through the early stages of dating

communication weirdness and you're on the other side. Things are moving right along. You are saddling up the horse to ride off into the sunset to Happily Ever After when . . . he vanishes. Poof! Gone without a trace. Last night he sent you a sweet "Good night, beautiful" text and conveniently left off the "Have a nice life." You go from talking multiple times a day and seeing each other multiple times a week to checking the sides of milk cartons for his face. *What went wrong?* Unfortunately, in these types of situations, you rarely get closure. Usually the guy just disappears into the night, never to be seen or heard from again, thereby leaving you with one heck of an unsolved mystery.

Despite all these issues, I am happy to report that a communication break*down* can sometimes lead to a break*through* instead of a break*up*. A girlfriend of mine has been seeing a guy who, at times, met criteria for all three of the points above . . . yet they worked through it, and just last week, he asked her to be his girlfriend! This is a true story and not an urban legend. So keep the faith, ladies! Keep being open, keep communicating, and keep being clear about what you want, and I truly believe that someday, somewhere, someone will come along who wants the same things as you. And all the guys who came before him will vanish from your mind faster than . . . well, the guys who came before him.

RULE TO Re-meme-ber

Ultimately, what it comes down to is this: if we don't believe that we are worthy of the very best love and life have to offer, and if we don't believe we are deserving of full-on, no-holds-barred, emotionally engaged, communicative partners, we will never attract those types of people to us. If we don't show up for ourselves, we will continue to attract the Houdinis and the breadcrumbers and the ghosters who don't show up for us either. If we don't communicate our needs out of fear that we aren't worthy of having them met, they will continue to go unmet. Here's the thing: you are worthy of someone who calls when he says he's going to call and texts when he says he's going to text and openly and honestly communicates his feelings to you. You are worthy of someone who REALLY, REALLY loves you. But YOU have to believe it to receive it.

You are worthy of someone who REALLY, REALLY loves you. But YOU have to believe it to receive it.

4

The Texting 411

Relationship or Textationship?

I still remember . . . *shudder* . . . a time before texting. *The Land Before Time*, some might call it. I didn't even get my first cell phone until I was eighteen, and that was still back in the T9 word days. Most millennials and Gen Z-ers have absolutely no idea what I'm referring to . . . and to be honest, I didn't understand T9 back then, and I still don't understand it to this day. As I recall, it was a really convoluted version of Autocorrect. And we all know that Autocorrect is drunk . . . so imagine if drunk Autocorrect had an even drunker uncle. That was T9 word.

Nowadays, I think society might cease to exist without texting. I text so much, and I use text lingo, emojis, and gifs (it will always be a hard *g* to me, like the word *gift*—I don't care what anyone says) so frequently to communicate, I struggled at times to write this book without wanting to insert an emoji every other sentence. It's the way we communicate now, and I don't see that changing anytime soon.

Even as recently as ten years ago, I remember spending *hours* on the phone with the person I was dating, especially in those early, heady days of falling for each other. We would talk into the wee hours of the night, then we both had to get up for work the next morning and were completely exhausted. But it was worth every yawn the next day to have the whole affectionate "You hang up!" "No, *you* hang up!" "No, *you* hang up!" back and forth for thirty minutes until we both decided that neither of us was hanging up. It feels like something really sweet and pure and beautiful has been washed away in the wave of modern technology. Texting is great and convenient and my preferred form of communication most of the time. But I just don't think you can connect and bond as deeply with someone when you're first getting to know them if every conversation takes place via text. That said, for the guys who randomly take it upon themselves to initiate a FaceTime call without first scheduling an appointment to do so like a normal person . . . please, for the love of all that is good and holy . . . stop this madness! If we haven't even met face-to-face yet, you haven't earned FaceTime-to-FaceTime privileges. And I am *not* going to answer your call with zit cream on my face and my hair looking like more of a hot mess than every movie character Johnny Depp has ever played.

I used to think that if a man texted and never called, that meant he was just not that into you. But the times, they are a-changing, and my thoughts on the subject have changed too. If I still felt that way, that would mean five out of the six guys I've dated over the past few years just weren't that into me. (Which, come to think if it, isn't that far off base.) Seriously, though, I believe that our ways of communicating have changed dramatically in the past decade, and convenience has trumped sentimentality. Much like movie-rental stores have gone extinct in favor of the convenience of binge-watching Netflix and Hulu (and all the other 10,497 streaming services) from the comfort of your own home, calling has gone extinct in favor of texting.

Is that a sign that we're not putting as much effort into cultivating our relationships as we once did? I used to think so. But it takes some serious work to come up with the perfect meme or gif for any given text-convo scenario . . . amirite?! The great thing about modern texting is that we have the wonderful invention of memes and gifs and emojis to liven up a conversation. The right gif or meme at the right moment? *Hilarious*. I have had text conversations with some of the guys I've dated that have caused me to actually LOL, like really loud, in public places. And there's nothing like finding a guy who can make you laugh, especially using nothing but a silly gif or meme. I still have screenshots saved on my phone of some of my more memorable and funny text conversations, not just with guys I've dated but with friends of mine, which is another little benefit of being a card-carrying member of the texting generation. If you're a sentimental person like me, you can save snapshots of your meaningful or funny or sweet conversations with people you care about to take out on a rainy day and laugh or smile at later. So there are lots of reasons to love texting and even arguments to be made that texting might actually bring us closer together instead of farther apart.

That said, what can texting tell us about whether or not someone is genuinely interested and invested in us? Since we can't see facial expressions or read body language via text, mixed signals can abound. And if we don't learn how to read the signs, we can easily find ourselves on the flip side of the relationship, feeling like most people did on the flip side of the movie *Cats*: dazed, confused, and wondering what the heck just happened to them.

So are his texting red flags all in your head, or is he in fact leaving the relationship on read? Here's how to know:

1. Is he engaged in regular conversation with you? Or are his texts random and sporadic? And are you the one always initiating the conversations? If you answered yes to the last two, he might be a breadcrumber. I once met a

guy on a dating app who would only text me, like, once a week. Since we had never met in person, it was completely baffling to me. Why bother to continue texting me at all? I mean, what was the point? Eventually, and not surprisingly, he tapered off communication until he finally vanished from my inbox completely. It might have been the slowest disappearing act from a Houdini that the world has ever seen. While your boo shouldn't be expected to text you all day every day (I mean, c'mon . . . we have actual lives that exist outside our phones, people), if you're not hearing from him on a fairly regular basis throughout the week at first and then throughout the day as things get more serious, he's almost definitely sharing the text wealth with someone else. (And you deserve to be the one showered with gifs.)

2. Are you spending time together in person, or is the relationship on a text-only basis? If the answer is the latter, I'm afraid that you, my friend, are not in a relationship at all . . . you're in a textationship. A new species that has evolved on the landscape of modern dating is a man (or woman, as I've heard from some of my guy friends) who subsists on texting alone and doesn't require or desire actual human interaction. There are many potential factors that play into this person's serial texting ways: They could already be in another relationship, and you're their unwitting side chick, they could be juggling so many different relationships that there aren't enough hours in the day to *meet* all the women they're texting, or they might be someone who simply prefers the impersonality of emojis over the intimacy of actual emotions. There's also always a chance you're being catfished. Whatever the reason, if they've made it clear that they have no intention of taking the relationship from text-level to next-level, it's

best to walk away now before your heart emoji turns into the broken-heart emoji.

3. Finally, did he break up with you through the virtual Post-It Note of a text message? (If you don't know this reference, there's an episode of *Sex and the City* where Carrie's boyfriend, Burger, ends their relationship by leaving her a four-word goodbye on a Post-It note.) I know the inclination when someone breaks things off in such an impersonal way is to seek answers and closure by asking—or even begging—for a face-to-face meeting. But here's the thing: this is one instance where you *do* have to believe the swipe because he just pulled the equivalent of swiping left on your entire relationship. If he can end things with you in such a cold, impersonal way . . . if he doesn't feel like he owes you the dignity of an in-person conversation . . . if he has texted his way right out of your life, then it's best to let him keep on walking. No one who cares for you and is worthy of you will ever give you this sort of *un*-ending. Just yesterday a girlfriend of mine texted her significant other of two months to ask him if they were still on for the movies last night. His response? "I've decided we're not a good fit." Welp, he got at least one thing right. He's not "fit" to be in a relationship at all and certainly not with my amazing, bossbabe friend. Anyone who gives you this kind of "badbye" is clearly a bad guy and completely unworthy of your character . . . or your characters.

While texting can make the early stages of dating trickier and murkier than they already are, if you look closely and are honest with yourself, your guy's intentions will eventually become clear. I truly believe that if a man is interested, genuinely interested, in taking things to the next level with you, the texting will eventually translate into face time—and no, not FaceTime—actual face time. If it doesn't, you might want to reconsider the "relationship." I mean, who wants to date their phone? You deserve a relationship with an actual person, and, no, Siri doesn't count. Give it a few weeks and enjoy the text flirting and talking to see how things evolve, certainly . . . but after a certain amount of time, if he's still only pushing buttons to communicate, it might be time to push End and walk away.

RULE TO Re-meme-ber

You don't have to be a detective to detect real, genuine interest. So, if you find yourself having to use a microscope to search for his feelings for you, chances are, they're not strong enough. What it boils down to is this: if someone genuinely wants to make an effort, they will. If they want to text you, call you, love you, and be with you, they'll do those things. And if they don't, they won't. No amount of asking, begging, bargaining, chasing, hoping, or wishing will change a thing. You deserve someone who *cannot wait* to text you and talk to you and spend time with you and get to know you and fall in love with you and sweep you off your feet. Please stop settling for halfhearted and lukewarm textationships instead of actual relationships. You, quite simply, deserve more. And it's sooooo much better to be alone than to be with someone who makes you FEEL alone.

It's sooooo much better to be alone than to be with someone who makes you FEEL alone.

5

Happily Never After

The Bad Date That Does Not Kill Us Makes Us Stronger

There are a few inevitabilities in life.

You will hit every green light in town when you're trying to either (A) eat and drive or (B) put on your makeup and drive.

Hangers will always multiply while socks vanish.

The roof of your mouth will always feel like it was left out in the sun too long the day after you eat your weight in Cookie Crisp. (Why, exactly, does Cookie Crisp make the roof of your mouth raw? That has always perplexed me.)

And if you're out here in this crazy little thing called modern dating for any amount of time, eventually you will experience a date that makes you question whether Ashton Kutcher has revived his hit MTV show, *Punk'd*, and is just waiting with his camera crew to pop up from the next booth where you're contemplating stabbing yourself in the eye with a steak knife just to escape the torture of the bad date that has befallen you.

In my history of using dating apps, I've met some truly amazing men. I've had some awesome experiences, some not-so-awesome experiences, and a handful of "You can come out now, Ashton" experiences. The stories I'm about to tell you fall into the last category, because I feel like it's always important on the modern dating journey to remind ourselves that we are going to have to kiss a few frogs to find our prince. And also to remember even on the worst, most miserable, most awkward date I've ever been on . . . I've rarely walked away from it without a valuable life lesson.

Not long after I started online dating, I ventured out on a first date—a lunch date—with one of my matches. It was a beautiful day and I was in great spirits—until I got to the restaurant, that is. I was able to pick out my date fairly quickly because it was a small restaurant, but my heart sank as I got closer and realized he had obviously used photos on his profile that were taken at least ten years (and about thirty or forty pounds) ago. *You guys.* I had been totally kittenfished! Now, let me clarify. This is not meant to be catty or mean or body/age shaming. I've gone out with men of all sizes and ages and body types. In fact, gym rats and guys who are overly obsessed with fitness/their body tend to drive me absolutely up the wall. But here's the thing: online dating is much like online shopping. The pictures need to be accurate. If I'm buying a pair of shoes online, I want to see pictures of the *actual* pair of shoes I'm buying, in their current state, scuffs and all, and then reserve the right to either accept them as is or move on. I don't want to see a picture of the shoes when you first bought them five years ago. That's not an accurate representation of what I'm getting. So, if you're going to do online dating of any kind, be honest about yourself. Yes, put your best foot forward with your most flattering images, but make sure they're images that are no more than a year old and that actually look like you. Otherwise, it feels dishonest. I don't ever want to show up to a date and have a guy not recognize me from my photos . . . and I don't want the same thing to happen to me.

Okay, back to my lunch date. Once I got past my initial shock, I decided to roll with things and see how the date played out. Welp, the date played out by him ordering my food *for* me. Because apparently the restaurant was also a time machine and we had traveled back to the year 1922. I'm an independent woman, and I like to order my own food, thank you very much. He ended up ordering a couple of things for me that I didn't even like, and while I continued to try to roll with things and be polite by choking down the food he'd ordered, I was growing increasingly skeptical/irritated. (Side note: I should have spoken up and told him I wanted to order for myself. This was early in my online dating journey, and I was still very much letting the swipe rule my life.)

The final strike came when he began hacking and coughing and, for lack of a better word, snarfling (yes, I realize I just invented a word) all over the food. Apparently he had a cold or allergies or something . . . but it got to the point where I almost needed an umbrella to defend myself and my food from the onslaught of saliva showers coming my way. It was bad, y'all. I tend to have a bit of a temperamental stomach anyway, so trying to eat my lunch while being hit with Hurricane Hacker was just too much for me, so I ended up barely touching my food. (Side note: Obviously all of this took place before the era of Covid-19, including the writing of this book. If someone hacked and coughed like this in a restaurant now, I imagine the restaurant would show them the door, and rapidly.) He even asked me in a rather accusatory tone, "Are you not eating because you're afraid I'm coughing on the food?" Well, duh, homie. Is the sky blue? Do cows say *moo*? Of course that's why I'm not eating THE FOOD THAT I DIDN'T EVEN GET TO ORDER MYSELF.

(Okay, stepping away from the caps lock key and taking a few deep breaths . . .)

After about an hour, I'd had all I could take and politely made my retreat from the restaurant. My only real consolation was thinking to myself, *There's no way I will hear from this guy again, because there's no way he thought that went well.*

Well (and you know what's coming), within ten minutes, I got a message from him asking me out on a second date.

I decided to wait until I got home and wasn't driving to craft a polite response, letting him down easy and letting him know I didn't feel a connection. In my opinion, honesty is always the best policy. I don't want to be led on or ghosted, and I don't want to do those things to anyone else.

Before I could even get home, however, he fired off a follow-up message (because apparently my immediate response was required, never mind the fact that I was driving thirty minutes home because I had agreed to meet him for lunch on his turf): "Never mind. I guess you were just using me for writing material."

Y'all. I *cannot.* I am so unable to *can* that my *can*s have taken leave of my body. My *cans* are currently on the side of a milk carton with "Have you seen us?" written in big, bold lettering.

Now, I know what you might say: "But, Mandy . . . you *are* writing about him, so you did use the situation for writing material."

Truth be told, I would have probably never written about this incident had he not been so unnecessarily rude and spiteful and passive-aggressive with that response. I would have just let it fade away and never mentioned it again, out of the goodness of my heart. I never like to feel like I'm unnecessarily calling anyone out or being hurtful. And that's not my intent here. My intent here is to help you know how to handle yourself when a bad date takes an even worse turn, and also to share with all of you my response to his hateful message.

And that was . . .

Nothing. I didn't respond. I simply unmatched from him and went about my merry way. Because sometimes it's better to just let things go than to try to get the last word. I could have written him back and roasted him for all the glaring faux pas he committed during our date, but it wasn't worth the time or energy or drama. Some things you've just gotta let go and let slide. And sometimes the best response is no response at all.

Next up in Mandy's Bad Date Hall of Fame, we have Rejection Guy. Rejection Guy and I met one night for dinner, and it took me all of about thirty seconds to see that he quite sullenly and angrily wore rejection on his sleeve. This date inspired me to establish my rule of only meeting for coffee on first dates. There is no point in risking hours of misery over dinner or even lunch if the two of you don't hit it off. It's best to keep the first meeting short and sweet, and then if it goes great, you can set up another date. That's a much better option than finding yourself contemplating whether you can fit through the tiny window in the ladies' room to make your escape.

Anyway, Rejection Guy told me within the first twenty minutes of meeting him that he had been fired from almost every job he'd ever had because his bosses hated him, his roommate hated him, and every girl he'd ever dated was a witch with a B and, oh yeah—they also hated him. And yes, he used that term. Over dinner. With a girl. On a first date. Obviously, I wasn't exactly seeing rainbows and shooting stars. More like landfills and litter boxes. It was *awful.*

As miserable as the evening was, it taught me a valuable lesson. Carrying around rejection is like walking around carrying an open smelly bag of garbage. It's unattractive, it's off-putting, and it permeates everything around you until no one can stand to be anywhere near you. We've all been rejected. We're all at least a little afraid of rejection. But choosing to tightly clench that rejection and make it your lifelong companion will keep you from ever finding an actual companion. Who knows if I would have been attracted to this guy or would have wanted to spend more time with him had he not carried around his rejection like a badge of honor . . . but now I'll never know. And I guarantee no one else will know, either, until he is willing to make some drastic changes. I feel for him, I do. I know the sting of rejection. But at a certain point, you have to stop blaming the world around you for your misery and start looking within to see what *you* can do differently. Most of the time it's as simple as just laying down the blame and the shame and taking responsibility for your own actions, feelings, and choices. By continuing to point the finger at everyone else for every little hurt and heartbreak and denial you've received, you only continue to invite more rejection into your life.

Here are a few more examples of classic frogs in Prince Charming's clothing from my colorful dating history:

Mr. Too Much, Too Soon (also known as a love bomber): You know who I'm talking about. We've all encountered him. You're sitting at dinner, gazing at your dreamboat, feeling the first-date butterflies, ready to get down to the preliminary getting-to-know-each-other talk, when he grabs your hand and tells you he's never felt this way before. Since the waitress hasn't even brought out the menu yet, you're thinking surely he must mean he's never felt such affection for a restaurant. By the time the salads have arrived, he's told you he thinks he's falling in love. As the waitress slides your steaks in front of you, he's calling his parents to invite them to dinner so they can meet his "soulmate." If he starts to fumble in his coat pocket and sink to one knee in front of you as you nervously start to nibble your dessert, it's time to scream, "Check, please!" and run—not walk—to the nearest exit. Because here's the cold, hard truth: if he's stalking you before the bill even arrives, there is a restraining order in your very near future.

Mr. Cheap: He's told you about what a great job he has, how he was promoted to senior vice president of the company in a week and a half . . . even how much is in his 401(k). Though you're not at all the type to be seduced by money, you can't help but be impressed by how successful he seems to be. So imagine your surprise when he takes you to Mr. Cluck's Chicken and whips out his Smart Card to get two entrees for the price of one. When the waitress asks, "Will this be together or separate?" he shrieks "Separate!" before the words even leave her mouth. When the check arrives and the waitress has forgotten to separate it, he pulls out his calculator to determine what your half of the $6.47 bill is. This is your signal to cash in your chips and walk because, hey—you really do gotta know when to hold 'em and know when to fold 'em. If a man doesn't at least offer to pick up the tab for the first date (after you do the polite check grab, of course), and if you're not worth even the cost of a wing and thigh to him, the relationship is probably not worth another second of your time.

Mr. Bad Kisser: You had a really great date. The conversation was good. There was no awkwardness or dead space or moments of silence that dragged on longer than a CVS receipt. You're thinking maybe this guy might even be a keeper . . . or at least worth trying a second date on for size. As you're standing at your door, nervously saying good night and figuring out the appropriate farewell ritual (shake hands? awkwardly hug it out? kiss on the cheek?), you're suddenly bombarded by two giant lips coming toward you with no way to escape. It's as futile as the *Titanic* trying to avoid the iceberg . . . it just ain't happening. You weren't even sure that you wanted to kiss at all on the first date, and now all of a sudden you're the recipient of more saliva than a newborn baby's bib. And the worst part is, he's an equal opportunity kisser—meaning he didn't just stop at your lips but is spreading the love to your cheeks, eyes, nose, chin—there's virtually no area of your face that's safe from this good-night kiss. Here's the cold, hard truth: the date might have been great, but a trip to the nightly saliva spa is going to get really old really fast. Somewhere along the way, someone gave Mr. Bad Kisser the idea that his kissing was actually *good*, and no amount of aversion therapy will convince him otherwise. So unless you're ready to be in a relationship with a Saint Bernard, it's clear this coupling is going to the dogs. Sometimes you just can't teach an old dog new tricks.

Is this parade of colorful characters an indictment against online dating? Absolutely not. That guy you meet at the bookstore or the one you bump into at the coffee shop or the one you lock eyes with while grabbing for the same Christmas tree at the Christmas tree farm (sorry, I've lapsed into Hallmark-movie speak again) could turn out to be just as green and warty and toad-like as anyone you cross paths with on a dating app. I've gone out on dates with guys that I met online that went completely smoothly. And while most of them didn't turn into love connections, some *did* turn into friendships. And if nothing else, they all helped me get some quality dating experience under my belt.

And the great thing about dating apps as opposed to meeting someone organically is this: on a dating app, you can simply unmatch and move on with your life without ever having to give out your phone number. No muss, no fuss. The app adds in an extra line of defense that you wouldn't have had otherwise. (Which brings me to another great rule of thumb: sometimes it's a good idea to hold off on giving out your phone number and only communicate on the app until you've met in person at least once. That way, 457 different random guys don't end up with your digits.)

So . . . yes, bad dates will happen in life, and snarflers and love bombers and bad kissers will come along, and sometimes you'll show up to a date hoping for a prince and meet a frog. But if you're tempted to lose heart—don't. There are some great guys out there (despite what your experiences or my experiences or statistics might tell you), and sometimes you have to weed through a few thorns to get to the roses. That's okay. Because all that really matters is *you showed up*. You tried. You put yourself out there. You were brave. And when it comes to modern dating . . . that's all you can do.

RULE TO Re-meme-ber

If you've been single for any amount of time, you've been out on at least a few less-than-ideal dates (that's my polite way of saying horrible dates), and the temptation can be to grow weary and frustrated and even disillusioned when true love seems so elusive. However, dear friends, there is no better way to figure out what you're looking for from life and especially from love than by experiencing what you're not. The big beautiful blessing of a bad date is that it always, always teaches you SOMETHING: what you don't want, won't accept, or won't ever again settle for. So be grateful for it all, because every sentence is a vital part of your story. And every wrong person pushes you one step closer to the right one.

The big beautiful blessing of a bad date is that it always, always teaches you SOMETHING: what you don't want, won't accept, or won't ever again settle for.

6

Why So Serious?

What If We Made Dating More about Having Fun Than Finding "the One"?

When you think about modern dating . . . like, really think about it . . . it's kind of hilarious. Can you imagine someday when you're like, eighty, and telling your grandchildren how you met your husband? "Grandma met Grandpa when she swiped right on a pic of him posing with a lion at the zoo. It was love at first swipe."

"What attracted you to him?"

"Oh, the way he gazed up at me . . . from his profile pic."

LOL! I've been talking with my single girlfriends a lot lately about the craziness of dating: comparing war stories, dissecting what we did wrong to make a relationship go south, laughing at some of the awkward situations we've found ourselves in . . . and with all the talk, I've reached what I feel is a very important conclusion.

Dating doesn't have to be so serious. In fact, it shouldn't be so serious. I mean, c'mon. It's a hoot!

When did we lose sight of that? I think of my own dating history, and I feel like I've done it all. Dated. Not dated. Waited on God. Kissed dating goodbye. Been in serious relationships. Been in long-distance relationships. I've received two pseudo-marriage proposals—and I mean "pseudo" in every sense of the word, because one was in the form of a drunken text message at 3:00 a.m. from the ex who inspired me to create my social media movement, The Single Woman, and the other was my most infamous ex, Mr. E, who took me to a jewelry store to show me engagement rings. Sounds romantic, right? Right up until I tell you that he showed me *lots* of rings but issued exactly zero marriage proposals. Yep, he took me to see engagement rings and then conveniently forgot to propose. (That entire jaw-dropping story is in my second book, *I've Never Been to Vegas but My Luggage Has*, if you wanna check it out.)

With the proverbial collection of gasp! shock! awe! LOL! moments I've racked up over the years, you would think I would have developed a better sense of humor about dating by now. And yet . . . I still take it too seriously.

A couple of years ago, I had a first date with a cute guy I had been eyeballing on Facebook for some time because he seemed like such a great catch. When he finally asked me out, I was super excited. So excited, in fact, I decided that absolutely nothing in my closet would be right to wear on said date. So I went on a shopping venture across town that would rival that of a celebrity stylist in search of the perfect gown for a client for the Oscars. And this was all for a *lunch date*. I wore myself out looking for the perfect outfit when my closet was full of suitable options.

Why did I feel so much pressure to be "perfect" for this lunch date? Probably because somewhere inside my head, I was thinking, "This guy is a really great catch, and really great catches don't come along very often, so I need to not mess this up." That is such a fatalistic approach! We have to stop treating every man we encounter as our last chance at happiness. Though I was authentically myself on the date, I look back at the experience and wish I hadn't put such intense pressure on myself or on the situation. And I wish I hadn't been so focused on looking like I'd just stepped out of a catalog and instead shown up wearing something from my closet.

The lunch went well (or so I thought), and we scheduled a second date . . . but he called and canceled the night before, and I never heard from him again. And you know what I was doing when he called to cancel? Shopping for shoes for our second date! I had full-blown, 100 percent drifted into "letting the swipe rule my life" territory. It's a good thing he canceled and I never saw him again, because I would have gone broke trying to look perfect for this guy. And why? He wasn't perfect. I'm sure he's a nice enough guy, but he had his own distinct set of issues, just like we all do. How often do we do that: build someone up to be the perfect guy or convince ourselves that because he looks "good on paper," he must be good for us? I think the problem is that once you get to a certain age, you start to look at dating less as an opportunity to have fun and meet new people and more as an audition for marriage. And that's far too much pressure and stress to put on yourself and on the situation. Not to mention on the guy.

I would like to propose that we change our attitude toward dating a little bit. I would like to suggest that we ease off all the expectations and the urgency and the seriousness and just have some fun. But how do we do that when society keeps drilling into our heads that we are more likely to be struck by lightning than to find love after a "certain age"? Here are a few tips:

- Take the pressure off by looking at dating as a great way to get to know new people and to have new experiences rather than expecting every man you meet to wife you up by the third date.

- Maintain your own identity, lifestyle, hobbies, and plans, and let dating complement that lifestyle instead of supplement it. You are single, and you know what single also means? *Free.* Free to travel, free to volunteer for charity organizations you believe in, free to take salsa lessons, free to splurge on that designer bag you found on Poshmark. When you have your own full, busy life, you're less likely to look for your value in the swipe.
- Hit the pause button on the frantic search for Mr. Right and just let yourself have some fun with Mr. *Right Now*! Not every person you date is going to be marriage material. Not every person you date is going to be "the one," or even in the running to be "the one." But every person you date *is* going to make you a little bit better at dating. A little more relaxed. A little more open to love. A little more certain about exactly what you're looking for. People are sent into our lives to teach us things we need to learn about ourselves . . . so look at dating as setting out a welcome mat for all sorts of little messengers who each have something new to show you about *you*.

I'm not suggesting that you juggle a dozen different guys and put your heart on the line, emotionally attaching yourself to every single one of them—far from it. You can play the field without trying to date the whole team! All I'm suggesting is that you try a bit to ease off the frantic search for happily ever after and start being happy *right now*. Allow yourself to date some "wrong" people. Spend time with people whose company you happen to enjoy, even if you don't see yourself marching down the aisle with them tomorrow. Maintain a healthy perspective on dating and stop setting your heart, your soul, your emotions, and especially your self-worth out on the line with every single person you encounter. When the time is right, you will know, and the safeguards you've put in place will fall away naturally. But until then—relax! Have fun! Be yourself in an outfit you didn't go out and buy specifically for the date. I have found, oddly enough, that most men tend to think women look a lot cuter in sweats and a ponytail than in a little black dress and Louboutins, anyway. (But ultimately, you should always dress for *you* and not for someone who may or may not end up becoming a significant part of your life.)

Most of all, no more letting the swipe rule your life. Stop looking for any dating app or anyone you might meet on a dating app to bring you the happiness and completeness you should be giving yourself.

Engage, converse, get out of your safe little comfort zone, and just get to know people with no other agenda than getting to know people. Approach dating from a place of, *Do I like him?* instead of always obsessing over, *Does he like me?* Sometimes we get so caught up in trying to make a good impression on someone we don't even stop to ask ourselves if *we* are impressed with *them*.

Finally, stop looking to every person to be the great love of your life, and allow dating to be a great adventure in your life. You'll likely make some amazing friends out of it, you'll definitely get some great stories out of it, and, who knows . . . having the time of your life just might lead you to the love of your life.

RULE TO Re-meme-ber

There is no timeline you must follow. You're not too late . . . you're not too early . . . you are just where you should be at this moment in your life, so relax. There's plenty of time to find love, there's plenty of time to get married, there's plenty of time to live happily ever after. And it starts by living happily *now* by embracing this version of yourself—this wild, unsettled, unfinished version of yourself. Every moment of your life and your journey is so precious and sacred, and it's so very, very okay that it is completely unique and entirely your own. You don't have to catch up to anyone or wait for anyone to catch up to you. You can simply go your own way and trust that everything meant for you will come in its perfect time, in its perfect way. You can stop viewing dating as something you *have* to do and start viewing it as something you *get* to do. You can stop frantically searching for "the one" and allow yourself to have a little fun.

Breathe. Relax. Trust. Let go. Laugh. Smile. *Live.* Your life is unfolding just as it should . . . so stop trying to skip ahead to the end, and enjoy the chapter you're in.

And while you're at it, remember that finding love is merely one chapter of your story. There is still an entire book of other crazy, beautiful, wild, funny, colorful, meaningful adventures to be lived.

You don't have to catch up to anyone or wait for anyone to catch up to you. You can simply go your own way and trust that everything meant for you will come in its perfect time, in its perfect way.

7

Jack It to Jesus

Stop Apologizing for Having High Standards (or Big Hair)

We all know that Dolly Parton is a national treasure . . . but something else I've always loved about Dolly is that regardless of how tiny she may be in stature, she doesn't shy away from heights. Not when it comes to her home (in the Smoky Mountains), not when it comes to heels, and definitely not when it comes to her hair. The way she has been known to describe her hair and how she likes to "jack it to Jesus" (get it as high and as close to heaven as possible) just *slays* me as a fan of big southern hair myself.

I would like to offer up a really wild suggestion. What if we channeled our inner Dolly and stopped being afraid of heights when it comes to setting the standard for our dating lives?

Behold an actual conversation I had with my mom recently regarding a man she thought I should go out with whom I had absolutely zero interest in:

"Mom, we are total opposites. He's Netflix and chill and I'm Amazon Prime and commitment. It would never work."

"But he's got *hair*!"

This is my mom's reasoning these days as to why I should date someone. This is what it's all come down to, ladies and gentlemen. Forty-one years on this earth, at least twenty-five solid years of those spent looking for my Prince Charming . . . and this is the lone standard I'm trying to meet? "He's got hair"?!

In my mom's defense, she just wants to see her daughter get married sometime before she's in a nursing home (or before I am). And she does make a valid point: a full head of hair on a man is a beautiful thing. It's increasingly hard to come by when you're dating in your thirties and about as rare as spotting the elusive purple ostrich of Patagonia by the time you reach your forties. (Okay, I totally made that up. There is no elusive purple ostrich of Patagonia, at least as far as I know. But you get the point. Hair is rare when dating over forty.) Still, though . . . this can't be all there is to it. Because I'm forty-one and single, does that mean I should have to compromise every standard I've ever had for myself and for the person I hope to marry, just so I can make it down the aisle at all costs? Does being single in your thirties and forties and beyond have to automatically equal settling, just to avoid winding up alone? And, if so, what exactly does that say about the value we place on our own life and our own solo journey?

Here's the thing: I like my life. I like my schedule. I like staying up late and sleeping in. I like the quiet, peaceful hours between midnight and 3:00 a.m. I also like choosing to turn in at 8:00 p.m. if I want to, and I like stretching across the entire bed when I do. Better yet, I like using the empty side of the bed for the books and magazines and other materials I read late into the night. Or for my laptop. Or for that stack of DVDs I'm making my way through (rewatching *Pretty Little Liars* for about the tenth time, currently).

I like running my fan at night as I sleep, and I like keeping the window up to let in the cool air in the fall so I can snuggle even deeper into my covers. I like that I don't have to listen to anyone snoring as I sleep, since I'm such a light sleeper that I can hear a mosquito sneeze in the next county. I like that if I wake up at 4:00 a.m. and want to eat cookies in bed, I can, and I won't wake anyone up in the process. I like that my DVR is filled with *This Is Us*, *Survivor*, and reruns of *The Golden Girls* and *Friends* rather than football or the news.

I like that my closet is filled (to the brim) with my clothes and shoes and that I don't have to save half the space for anyone else's clothes and shoes. (I especially like this.)

I like that I can eat cold pizza for breakfast and cereal for dinner if I choose to. I like that I can flip the two meals without concern that someone won't like my random tastes. I really like that I can use my kitchen cabinets for storage space rather than for dishes or canned foods. I like that I don't own a garlic press, nor do I know how to use one. I like that I have no need to know that right now.

I like that I choose my own bedtime, my own alarm clock setting, my own home décor, my own vacation spots, my own TV channels, my own meals, my own *life*. I like that I'm only thinking and planning for one. I like that I have multiple remote controls and no clue what they go to, but I'm afraid to toss them out because they could be connected to a device that I might someday want to use again . . . and I control them all.

I like that I can sit on my balcony on a cool autumn night with a blanket and a cup of hot cocoa and talk to God for hours, because I don't have anywhere else to be or anyone else to be with. I like that my heart belongs to Him and is safe with Him. I like that He is the only entity I feel the need to consult with before making big life decisions . . . and I like that I have the luxury of a deeply intimate walk with Him, because He has my undivided attention and undistracted devotion. I'm pretty sure God really likes that too.

So, after giving it all very careful consideration . . . I don't think I'm merely settling for my life. I think I've chosen it.

Yes, I want to be married someday. Maybe even someday not too far from now. I want to be a mom someday. I want to have a family, a tribe, a home team. But none of those desires discount the value of my life currently, just as it is. And my life is certainly worth way too much to just settle for the first man that comes along. I don't want to escape my life. And I don't want love to be an escape. I want it to be a sweet, beautiful respite.

I don't know about you . . . but I didn't wait this long and come this far to give up and settle for "okay." Or even for "good." Just "good" or "okay" is not going to cut it for me when it comes to the person I spend the rest of my life with. And I'm not going to apologize for that. I think that past the age of about thirty, single women with standards are too often labeled as too picky, too high maintenance, too hard to please, or a diva—all because we happen to know what we want and we're not going to settle for less. Well . . . I say, no more. We have to stand up and own our right to jack our standards to Jesus and be vigilant about who and what we allow into our lives. Especially as it relates to who we invite to share our lives.

Does this mean I think you should stubbornly refuse to give any guy a chance who doesn't look like Channing Tatum? Or that you should dismiss every guy who's a little shorter than you had hoped or blonder than you had visualized or older or younger than you had planned? No. There certainly should and needs to be flexibility and openness to the idea that the person you choose to spend your life with might not fit some preconceived mold or check every single box you have for him. There does have to be a willingness to compromise when it comes to the fine print. But the big things—Is he loyal and honest and kind? Does he have goals and dreams and ambition? Does he do what he says he'll do and follow through and keep commitments and show up for you? and so on and so forth—those are areas in which you have a right to stand tall and firm on your standards and not back down. Because here's the thing: yes, singleness can be a little lonely. It can be a little sad. It can be difficult and awkward, and let's be real: it just plain sucks at times. But nothing . . . and I mean *nothing* . . . is lonelier or sadder or more challenging than waking up one morning to find yourself trapped in a relationship with someone who is wrong for you, simply because you compromised your standards to avoid winding up alone. (Or because you chose him simply because he has hair.)

It's time to tell the world that, yes, we are single; yes, we have standards; and, *no* . . . we won't apologize for it. Because high standards don't signify a diva. They signify a woman who knows what she's worth.

RULE TO Re-meme-ber

You're allowed to have high standards. You're allowed to love yourself. You're allowed to believe that you are worthy of the very *best* in love and life. And you're allowed to not apologize for any of it.

Expecting to be treated well does not make you hard to love. Having boundaries does not make you hard to love. Refusing to settle for less than the best does not make you hard to love.

I'm not sure at what point we decided that a woman unwilling to compromise her standards and settle for less than the best is difficult, but can we cancel that archaic notion, please? Along with the idea that a confident woman is full of herself or that a woman who knows what she wants is a diva. It's not unreasonable to want to be treated well and to refuse to put up with nonsense. Never apologize for being the strong, confident, bold, self-assured bossbabe that you are. You fought *way* too hard to become her.

Expecting to be treated well
does not make you hard to love.
Having boundaries does not make you hard
to love. Refusing to settle for less than
the best does not make you hard to love.

8

Fifty Shades of Gray Area

Why a Situationship Will Never Become a Relationship

Now it's time for a pop quiz!

Who can tell me how the Modern Dating Dictionary defines a *situationship*?

You! You there in the front.

"A situationship is a romantic situation that is more than a friendship but less than a relationship. Basically, the gray area or purgatory of modern dating. Some people linger in situationships for years, *waiting and hoping to hit the tipping point into Love Town, but unfortunately, most situationships never leave the city limits of Ambiguous, population 2."*

Nicely done! You guys are paying attention.

Okay, back to our regularly scheduled program.

Long before I ventured into the world of online dating or dating apps, and right smack dab in the midst of a self-imposed five-year dating hiatus, I met a guy on Twitter. Yep, you can actually meet people on social media. I've had two or three situationships that were spawned from various social media platforms.

This guy and I—we'll stick with our theme of *Friends* characters and call him Ross Geller—started following each other on Twitter and then started tweeting back and forth to one another, and then one day . . . it happened.

He slid into my DMs.

At first as a friend . . . a good friend . . . and then something that felt like a little more. We talked a lot, laughed constantly, and over the course of almost six months, developed a connection that felt really, really special. He lived in another state, so we never met face-to-face, but the thread of authenticity and humor and honesty that ran through our conversations made me feel closer to him than some people who I saw on a regular basis. It was good. And it made me happy. And slowly, a little bit at a time, it opened me up to the idea of maybe, possibly wanting to date again. For whatever reason, I felt safe with Ross Geller, and I began to let someone in for the first time in years. It wasn't *love* . . . but it was *like*. Strong, deep, sincere *like*.

The problem was, Ross Geller confided in me about other women and didn't seem entirely invested in me romantically, even though we literally communicated all day every day via text and chatted on the phone almost every night. Since I had been out of the game for so long, I didn't have enough experience with dating to fully understand that we were stuck smack dab in the middle of Fifty Shades of Gray . . . Area. What was happening between us might have mildly resembled a relationship, but it wasn't a relationship. It was a situationship.

I must have been picking up on some sort of weird vibe . . . because my gut felt unsettled. And since I was starting to develop feelings for him, I knew I had to get to the bottom of our situation(ship) and figure out exactly where he stood before I let myself fall for someone who might not be ready to catch me.

I was nervous. It felt awkward to have a "Where is this going?" talk with someone who lived nine hours away and whom I had never even met in person.

So . . . I did what any sensible girl would do. I turned to my bath bomb for answers. You know what I'm talking about. The giant ball that you drop into your bath water and it fizzes and makes the water delightfully pink or sparkly or floral-scented or all of the above.

"What?" you're probably asking. *"Mandy has totally lost it this time."*

We'll get to that in a minute. But first, here's the thing: truth can come to us at any time, any place, in any form or fashion if we have eyes to see and ears to hear. Truth can arrive on a regular Tuesday morning. It can arrive in the mail. It can arrive via a phone call. It can arrive when we're not even looking for it at all. If you're open and you're willing to recognize it when it arrives . . . it can find you anywhere.

Yes, even through a fortune-telling bath bomb.

Now to explain that part. The bath bomb arrived as an item in a subscription box of beauty products I received every month. The instructions indicated that you should ask it a question, and when you dropped it into your bath water and it fizzled down, the answer would be revealed. Sort of the Magic 8-Ball of bath bombs. I should insert here that I don't put any stock in fortune-telling. But the day that box arrived, I was at a crossroads with Ross Geller and searching for clarity.

And sometimes clarity comes to us in funny ways.

"Will Ross Geller and I ever really date?" I asked, then tossed the bath bomb into the water.

A few minutes into my bubble bath, the bath bomb dissolved and the answer came.

As I read the three words, I realized I had known the answer in my gut long before a fortune-telling bath bomb gave it to me.

Not gonna happen.

Welp. There it was . . . spelled out for me.

A few days later, Ross Geller spelled it out even clearer. (*"Clearer than a fortune-telling bath bomb?"* you might be asking. *"Not possible!"*)

Ross Geller said he felt something for me . . . but not enough of a something to take our relationship to the next level (actually meeting in person). And that hurt. Gosh, it hurt. I couldn't understand how someone who had invested almost six months and countless phone calls, hundreds of texts, and a million laughs could so easily dismiss the idea that there might be something real between us. Of course, he was younger than me . . . still at an age I remember well as not fully being able to understand how rare it is in this life to find someone who makes you laugh not just some of the time but most of the time. It takes age and years and lots of life experience to grasp that there won't be endless opportunities to make that kind of connection. And I learned a long time ago that it does no good to wait around on someone's feelings to catch up to yours. So I had no choice but to move on, to release what almost/maybe/kinda was and accept that it would never be. Our situationship was never going to blossom into a relationship. It was, as the bath bomb said, *not gonna happen.*

Here's the thing, friends:

If a guy is confiding in you and asking for your advice about other women . . . it's probably not gonna happen.

If you have a text-only relationship with a guy . . . it's probably not gonna happen.

If a guy is completely and admittedly emotionally unavailable . . . it's probably not gonna happen.

If it's been years and you're still just hanging out instead of dating . . . it's probably not gonna happen.

If your Facebook status says "In a relationship," and his says "Single" . . . it's probably not gonna happen.

If you feel like you need to seek the wisdom of a fortune-telling bath bomb about the future of your relationship . . . it's probably not gonna happen.

You see, I had known all along it was probably never gonna happen. It just took having it literally spelled out in front of me for me to accept it.

Our gut always knows. Our heart always knows. Our intuition always knows. It's up to us whether we choose to listen.

You know right now that situationship you're in is never going to magically transform into a relationship. You already know. You might be banging your head against walls in frustration or praying for a sign or asking every friend you have for advice . . . but the truth is, you already know. If you're willing to see and admit the truth, you'll find that you already know it—with or without a fortune-telling bath bomb. How do you know? Because a situationship rarely graduates to a relationship. Some men are perfectly happy to let things linger in the gray area for as long as we'll allow it. In the gray area, they get to enjoy the benefits of our company without any of the responsibilities of a real relationship. And if you never speak up and let them know you want and need and deserve more . . . honestly, you can't even get mad at them for not giving you more. Those are your two options: speak up and ask for what you want—a real relationship—or walk away without the relationship but with the valuable lessons that the "almost" relationship taught you. Because no one ever leaves you empty-handed. Everyone who crosses our path has something to teach.

So, what did my situationship with Ross Geller teach me? After a few days of thinking it all over . . . it hit me. He was never meant to be my great love. Or even a love at all. He was just meant to get me ready for it.

I wasn't open to love or dating or relationships or any level of intimacy for a really long time. My heart was closed tighter than a drum. After six months of my almost/not-quite relationship with Ross Geller, I was open, and so was my heart. My life colliding with that of a guy hundreds of miles away, whom I never met face-to-face, changed everything for me.

You see, not everyone's lives that intersect with ours intersect for the reasons we want them to, or *think* we want them to. Sometimes the seemingly most obvious reason isn't the reason they're in our lives at all. But that doesn't make their purpose any less special, important, or necessary. We're so quick to dismiss someone who hurts us as a mistake or a waste of time or a hard-earned lesson, but what if . . . just what if . . . they're actually a blessing? One we may not unwrap today or even tomorrow but eventually we'll look back on as the moment that changed everything for us?

Ross Geller was my moment. And I will always be grateful for him. I haven't talked to him in years, but I hope he knows how grateful I am for the laughs, for the conversations, and, yes, even for The End.

Love isn't always black and white, as I once thought. Neither are relationships and dating, for that matter. My situationship with Ross Geller taught me that.

But love is also not meant to be a constant struggle. A constant question. Constant angst and turmoil and confusion and questions and doubts and seeking the wisdom of bath bombs.

The answer is always much clearer than we think or are willing to admit to ourselves.

Sometimes we just need it spelled out for us.

Sometimes something as seemingly insignificant as a fortune-telling bath bomb can help us see the truth that's been staring us right in the face the entire time.

What is meant to be ours will eventually be ours, and what is not . . . no matter how hard we try . . . will never be.

There's a peace in accepting that truth.

RULE TO Re-meme-ber

Words do not = actions, potential does not = reality, and situationships do not = relationships. You are worthy of someone who backs up their words with actions, who doesn't just tell you but shows you, who doesn't just have POTENTIAL to be a great guy . . . he IS a great guy. Please stop settling for almost, not-quite, halfway love. You deserve whole love, not skim love. Let those guys who want boyfriend privileges without the title or responsibilities go, and hold out for the one who will jump all the way off the high dive of love and into the deep end with you. *Because you are worthy.* And dust settles . . . you don't.

You are worthy of someone who backs up their words with actions, who doesn't just tell you but shows you, who doesn't just have POTENTIAL to be a great guy . . . he IS a great guy.

9

Not-So-Trivial Pursuit

Five Reasons Why You Should Never Chase a Guy

I consider myself a very evolved, independent, strong woman. I am a steel magnolia . . . I am no one's shrinking violet. And I don't need a man to chase me around endlessly or to doggedly pursue me while I feign disinterest in order to play hard to get. I'm actually not a fan of game playing at all. Once you hit forty, you're kinda over all the childish nonsense. These days, the only game I'm interested in is Scrabble. Or Heads Up! (Now, that game is just good times.)

All that said, I am also very much a traditionalist when it comes to dating. I don't need to be rabidly pursued, but I do prefer that the man make the first move. I prefer that the man be the initiator of at least the first date. Because I view dating as a dance, I prefer that the guy take the lead; not all the time but the majority of the time, especially in the early stages of dating. I'm not afraid to ask a man out, and I've been known to do it, but it's not my preference.

Why? Because I've never had good results when I've been in a dating situation where I was the primary instigator. Usually when I'm the primary instigator, it's a pretty clear sign that he's just not that into me. I don't know about you, but I've never known a man who didn't go after something he *really* wanted. Maybe you feel differently, and that's totally cool! If so, feel free to skip ahead to the next chapter. No hard feelings. I promise.

Modern dating can be extremely tricky. And by *tricky*, I mean often infuriating, frustrating, and about as clear as the meaning of those Matthew McConaughey car commercials. No one's dating anymore; they're hanging out. And in the midst of all this super casual "hanging out," signals and wires and intentions seem to have gotten crossed. Instead of men being engaged and taking initiative and making an effort to woo women, a lot of men seem to be sitting back, waiting on women to woo *them*. It's almost like, while the women have been working extra hard at dating, the men have taken an extended leave of absence. And it's causing all sorts of chaos.

Now, please don't make me launch into some diatribe about how men are natural hunters and gatherers and are genetically programmed to be the initiators of relationships (because it's true, but I don't feel like doing the research to prove it). And please don't misunderstand me either. I'm not suggesting we, as women, sit around sniffing our smelling salts like Scarlett O'Hara or play the hapless, helpless female in need of a big, strong man to come and rescue us. That's not my point here at all. My point is this: a lot of men seem to have forgotten how to make a genuine effort when it comes to dating because we ladies are making all the effort for them. And in my humble opinion, a relationship that begins as a result of a woman frantically chasing around after a man doesn't tend to have a happy ending. I know this because I'm forty-one years old and I can say with full confidence, and with years of dating experience under my belt, that anytime I have chased a man, the relationship has gone nowhere fast. When I sit back and relax and stay open and receptive to the relationship without doggedly pursuing it, it has always, always, always worked out better. Because if I make my interest known without overkill and the guy doesn't make a move, then I have my answer. And, by the way, I consider myself a strong, confident bossbabe. But part of being a strong, confident bossbabe is knowing your heart, your time, and your company are worth being wooed and pursued. I mean . . . I *want* to be wooed and pursued! (And I'm not ashamed to admit that.) Don't you?

Now, let's define what exactly I mean by *chasing*, just so we're clear. I absolutely believe that making your interest known and clear is a beautiful and even necessary thing. Men need to know that we're into them as much as they are into us. I don't consider texting a man first, asking a man out, or being 100 percent open and demonstrative about your feelings *chasing*. Again, I'm never about being coy or cagey or playing games. *Chasing* is when you're daily blowing up his phone and he's breadcrumbing you with one or two vague responses a day. *Chasing* is when you've asked him to hang out five times to his one. *Chasing* is when you are making *all* of the effort, and he is making none.

If you've lost months or years of your life to endlessly pursuing a man who always seems to stay one step ahead of you . . . here are five reasons why you should stop chasing that guy:

1. It's humiliating, exhausting, and downright bad for your self-esteem. It's impossible to feel good about yourself if you're willing to trade in your dignity for a pair of running shoes in order to chase after any man—especially one who doesn't seem all that interested. And your dignity and self-esteem are worth way too much to surrender for anyone or anything.
2. If you have to chase him, ladies, here's the cold, hard truth: he doesn't want to be caught. A man who wants to be with a woman will always run *toward* her, not away from her.

3. He's clearly not that great of a guy. Why? Because a man of character would stop dodging, evading, and being shady and sit down with you face-to-face to tell you honestly that he doesn't want to be with you. He wouldn't keep playing games with your heart or keep you hanging around as his backup plan.
4. You are missing out on the things and people and relationships that *are* meant for you by wasting all your time, energy, and emotions on the things that are not. When you stop chasing the things that aren't for you, you give the things that *are* a chance to catch up to you. But as long as you're caught up in the drama of a hopelessly frustrating and seemingly endless pursuit, you literally have blinders to all the amazing things (and people) already staring you right in the face.
5. Even if you catch him, you won't really ever have him. I've learned this firsthand, the hard way. You can have someone's physical presence there with you, and their heart can still be light-years away. On the bright side, the really amazing thing that sometimes happens by catching someone you've been chasing for so long is it finally opens your eyes to why it was never meant for you to catch them at all. Because sometimes it takes getting everything you ever thought you wanted to fully understand it's nothing you need and far from what you deserve.

In closing, be open, be clear, be communicative, be engaged, don't be afraid to be bold and text, call, or ask a man out first . . . but please, by all means . . . stop chasing him if he keeps running. Something better is coming! You are worth being wooed and pursued. It's time to resign from any relationship that makes you feel like you have to hustle for anyone's time, love, and attention.

The only man you should be chasing is the ice cream man on a hot summer day.

RULE TO Re-meme-ber

You will never have to fruitlessly chase any relationship that is truly meant for you. You will never have to tell the right man how to act. You won't have to ask him to show up for you or meet you halfway or be a gentleman or put in effort. You won't have to beg him to be excited about you. You won't have to do all the planning and the calling and the texting and the orchestrating of a relationship that's truly meant to be. If your "relationship" feels like a job . . . it's time to resign immediately. Love should not be that hard. It just shouldn't. You deserve someone who makes you feel special regularly, who matches your effort, who makes you smile rather than cry. You deserve someone who's *all in*. Stop settling for crumbs, beautiful one. You are worth the whole entire meal.

If your "relationship" feels like a job . . . it's time to resign immediately. Love should not be that hard. It just shouldn't.

10

Who You Gonna Call?

How to Keep a Ghost from Haunting You

G*hosting.*

The most commonly used dating term, the most commonly experienced dating phenomenon, and a part of our daily vernacular in a way that, ten years ago, we never would have or could have imagined. In fact, if someone from a decade ago picked up this book and saw all the mentions of ghosting, they would be sure they had picked up a book about a haunted house.

Anyone in the modern dating world in any capacity has been ghosted. Some of us have been visited by more ghosts than Ebenezer Scrooge. You know the drill. You've been out a couple of times, you're starting to really vibe, things seem to be going great, you're texting every day, you've maybe even had an elusive phone call or two . . . when all of a sudden—*poof!*—he vanishes into thin air and into the night, leaving you wondering what you did wrong or what could have happened to scare him away. Sometimes you even check obituaries because only death is a suitable excuse for him falling off the face of the earth.

Several years back, I ran into an ex and we started reminiscing about old times (I have an unfortunate habit of recycling my exes, but more on that later) . . . and before I knew what was happening, he had asked me out for Friday and Saturday of the upcoming weekend, and I had said yes to both. (In hindsight, I can see that was a major red flag. I mean, double-booking someone you haven't seen in years? *Way* too much, too soon.) We chatted all week, and when Friday rolled around, he texted to confirm he would pick me up at 7:00. Welp . . . 7:00 came and went, and no date. 7:15, no date. 7:30—yep, you guessed it—still no date. I shot him a text: "Hey! You on your way?" No response. He had fallen off the face of the earth. And I was completely flummoxed.

Obviously, he was a no-show on Saturday night too, and he failed to respond to phone calls or numerous texts. My fury started to turn to concern. Was he still . . . alive? This was somewhere between the fall of Myspace and the rise of Facebook, so there was no social media profile for me to scope out and see if he was okay. So I did the only thing I knew to do: I started scanning the obituaries.

Spoiler alert: he wasn't dead. But he *was* a ghost.

I would love to say that's the only time I've been ghosted, but in the era of modern dating and dating apps and swiping right and left and seemingly endless possibilities, it's entirely possible to get ghosted two to three times a week.

In an age of endless forms of communication, never has it been easier for people—yes, even friends—to excommunicate themselves from our lives. I've been ghosted by friends too. Just last year, a friend who was very near and dear to me disappeared from my life. I'm at the place in my life where I don't want to do all the work anymore when it comes to friendships or relationships, so I decided to just let it go and see what happened. Turns out, that friendship was a dead plant I had been watering, because I never heard from her again. I don't want to feel like I'm making all the effort, doing all the inviting, always reaching out and asking and planning and coordinating in my relationships, romantic or otherwise. It's exhausting. And it leaves me wondering, *If I stopped doing all the work, would this person still be in my life?* And if the answer to that question is no, then was the relationship ever really that strong to begin with? The good news is, I've learned more than a little bit about letting go. I don't want to hold on to people who don't want to be in my life. And if we lose friends or romantic prospects simply because we are no longer willing to carry the weight of the entire relationship on our backs, is it really a loss? I think some losses are really gains in that we gain back time and energy we were investing in the wrong people and reclaim parts of ourselves that we lost in the frantic effort to stay in the life of someone who wasn't doing anything to keep us there. Not to mention the great big open space we now have to fill with other people who love our company and want to invest in us!

My adventures in dating have taught me a lot about letting go too. The hard truth I've learned is that some guys are going to disappear with no explanation, and there's nothing I can do about it and no point in trying to understand it. Sometimes I think a meet-up or a date went really well and then I never hear from the guy again. It's not always going to make sense, and I'm not always going to get an answer or closure. That's just life.

What I've learned from my own experiences and from talking to my guy friends about why men ghost is this: sometimes it's just easier for someone to vanish than to provide a complicated and awkward explanation about *why* they're vanishing. Typically, when a guy goes *poof* into the night after a date or two, it's for one of a few reasons: either he's not into you, or at least not into you *enough*, he's into someone else, or he's decided to go back to an ex. (Or in some cases, he never left the ex to begin with and was lying to both of you and, in that case, good riddance. Actually, in *all* these cases, good riddance!) The truth is, you may never know why someone chooses to disappear from your life, but the fact that they disappeared tells you everything you need to know about them and about the relationship.

Whether it's a friendship or a relationship . . . here are a few ways to keep a ghosting from haunting you:

1. Ask yourself, *Is there any way I am overlooking an infraction on my part? Did I do anything wrong? Is there something I need to own up to and apologize for? Did I alienate this person in any way?* If so, do what you need to do to make it right. Sometimes when we get honest with ourselves, we realize that our own actions played a role, however minor, in the other person's retreat. However, I will say this: when someone completely vanishes from your life without a trace, typically there was nothing you did to cause it and nothing you could have done to stop it.
2. Make peace with the fact that you may never know why they disappeared, stopped texting, stopped calling, and never talked to you again. Maybe they were going through something in their own lives that caused them to isolate themselves. Maybe another friend or relationship came along and distracted them. Maybe they were intimidated by you and didn't see a place for themselves in your life (more on this later). Or maybe it was none of the above or all of the above. The point is . . . you'll likely never know. You can beat your head repeatedly into a wall trying to figure out the un-figure-out-able, or you can simply let go and move on with your life.
3. Realize that as horrible as this ghosting feels, this person's retreat from your life does not have to devastate you. You have other options, both in love and in friendship. Look around at the amazing people already in your life who *do*

> make an effort to be there. Hey! Now you have more time to spend with them. And more time to get out there and make new friends or meet new love interests. Be proud of yourself for being willing to put yourself out there and try new things and meet new people. You ventured outside your comfort zone and took a chance and that is *awesome*!

At the end of the day, know that ghosting says nothing about you and everything about the other person. If they couldn't take the time to explain why they needed to exit stage left, they're not worthy of a starring role in your life. Or even a bit part, for that matter. Don't hold a place for them. Move on to all the people and relationships and friendships that are rewarding, life-giving, and always reciprocal. They are out there, I promise. You just might have to swipe right or left a few times to find them.

RULE TO Re-meme-ber

You have to stop letting the swipe rule your life by equating a man's behavior with your worth. How he acts or doesn't act says way more about him than it does about you. Sometimes guys ghost and disappear and you never hear from them again and it makes zero sense. But unless you're acting needy or clingy, or you're getting way too attached and too serious, too fast and scaring him off, it's not about you at all. This is just the modern dating game. HIM disappearing doesn't mean YOU'RE not "worthy." It means he wasn't the right person for you. Not everyone you date is the right person. In fact, there are a lot more wrong ones than right ones! Like we talked about in chapter 1, you have to master the art of catch and release. If they act up or ghost or are halfhearted—release them and move on. But stop taking it as an indication of your worth, because the two things are completely separate. And if you don't know that, then you need to step away from dating and go to therapy and do the hard work on yourself until you are so secure in who you are, no one can shake it. There was a time when I allowed rejection to cause me to question myself too, but I ultimately decided I wasn't going to allow dating or any man or anyone on this planet to make me feel less than. *It's almost never about you.* Your worth is a fixed point and doesn't change based on someone's inability to see it. Now go forth and date in power, gorgeous!

HIM disappearing doesn't mean YOU'RE not "worthy." It means he wasn't the right person for you. Not everyone you date is the right person.

11

The Ex-Files

Is He Bringing His Past into Your Present?

Okay, so we've talked about ghosting and why men do it. One of the great big, huge contributing factors to ghosting is . . . the ex-files. No, not that creepy show from the '90s that made a comeback a few years ago but the actual ex-files. As in your current boo's ex-boo.

I have dated a wide array of men in all stages of post-relationship: Years. Months. Weeks. I have dated guys who have been through messy divorces and guys who are still going through messy divorces (doing the latter is a *major* mistake). I've dated men who told me they were separated and finalizing their divorce and, come to find out, they really weren't. I've dated men who had just gotten out of serious relationships and others just out of casual relationships. I've dated guys who are on good terms with their ex and guys who are on bad terms with their ex. I've done the research and made all the mistakes so you don't have to. And what I've observed in all my many dating experiences is that the ex-factor is *strong*. Like Bermuda Triangle strong. It's human nature to have a soft spot for your ex, but there's a difference between a soft spot and a weak spot. A soft spot is "Hey, we used to date and a part of me will always care about you and wish you the best." A weak spot is "Hey, we used to date and I'm still in love with you and I wish we were still together and you're totes still the wallpaper on my phone."

It's always good to take at least a passing peek through the ex-files before entering into any new relationship. And by that, I don't mean stalking his ex's Instagram feed. (Perish the thought of accidentally liking one of her photos from three years ago!) I'm talking about having an open and honest conversation with your new boo about where things stand with their ex-boo. Do they have kids together? Are they in communication regularly about the kids or for any other reason? Are they on good terms? Obviously, this conversation should not take place until you have a fairly established dating situation, as it's not advisable or even appropriate to bring up the ex on the first few dates. And if they bring up their ex on the first or second date, especially if it's in a negative or derogatory way—*run*.

If you're officially dating, exclusive or otherwise, and he acts touchy in any way at the mention of his ex, it's possible that he's still carrying a torch and just waiting for the first sign that she's ready to welcome him back into the fold. Here are a few warning signs that the ex-files might have your new man a text away from bringing his past into your present:

1. Timing. Is he six months out of his last relationship or six days? I typically have a rule that I won't date anyone who hasn't been out of a serious relationship for at least six months. I've been guilty of breaking that rule, and every single time, I've ended up with a broken heart as a result. Nobody wants to be a rebound, so no matter how charming he is, if his breakup happened five minutes ago . . . he's

swimming precariously close to the relationship Bermuda Triangle and is in danger of being sucked back in.

2. Relationship status. Is he single? Not "separated" or "finalizing a divorce" or "it's complicated" but completely and totally single? No matter how "over" he says the marriage is or how long he has been living apart from his ex or soon-to-be ex, until the divorce is 100 percent final, there is always a chance he will go back. Especially if there are kids involved.
3. Proximity to the ex. Is he uncomfortably close to his ex? Not in a healthy, "We're on good terms" kind of way but in a cringey, "We're attached at the hip" sorta way? Obviously, if he has children with her, they are going to communicate regularly, and you have to respect and honor that. (Kids always come first.) But there's a big difference between touching base about the kids and having hours-long heart-to-hearts or even text convos about personal matters. If your gut feels off about the vibe he has with his ex, pay attention to it. In this case, two's company, three's a crowd . . . so if you feel like the outsider in your own relationship, they are probably headed for Reconciliation Station and it's time for you to get off at the next exit.
4. Constant chatter. Does he talk about his ex constantly? Does he compare you to her? Does he defend her to you? People talk about what they're thinking about, so if her name is constantly on his lips, then she's not far from his heart and mind, and it's only a matter of time before she gets out of his dreams and into his car. (Are y'all too young for that reference? Surely not. If so, Google it.)
5. Social media status. Does his relationship status still say "Married" or "In a relationship"? Does he still have her photos plastered all over his social media pages

or hanging around his house? When someone has moved on from a relationship, they don't typically want constant reminders of their ex splashed across their Facebook feed or framed on the bedside table. If you are his number one, you—not his ex—should be his #WomanCrushWednesday.

These are just a few signs that your hot new man might still be carrying a torch for his ex. Ultimately, it comes down to your intuition. Your gut *always* knows. Listen to it. Pay attention to the red flags. Don't hesitate to heed the warning signs and walk away before you get any further attached. You deserve someone who is 100 percent ready and available and present and not still pining away for the past.

And while you're at it, make sure you're not still pining away for yours either. Are your own ex-files in order? It's important to check yourself too. Are you at least four to six months out of your last serious relationship? Did you give yourself time to heal from your last big heartbreak? Or are you rushing headlong into this new relationship to forget about your ex or worse—to make him jealous? The ex-files can make or break a new relationship, so before you open a whole new book with someone, make sure you've both closed the last one.

RULE TO Re-meme-ber

Where there's smoke, there's usually fire . . . so if you suspect your new love might still carry a spark for his ex-love, he probably does. But here's the thing: it's always better to know sooner rather than later. And that's why it's so important to set boundaries and have safeguards in place with your dating life so that you don't find yourself madly in love with someone who can't take his eyes off the rearview mirror long enough to see the beautiful view right in front of him. Establish a game plan for yourself before you venture onto the first dating app. Example: You won't date anyone who hasn't been divorced for at least a year or been out of a serious relationship for at least six months. Then stick to it. It might leave you with fewer options to choose from . . . but it will also leave you with fewer chances to wind up with a broken heart.

It's so important to set boundaries and have safeguards in place with your dating life so that you don't find yourself madly in love with someone who can't take his eyes off the rearview mirror long enough to see the beautiful view right in front of him.

12

Like Attracts Like

If You're Unavailable to You, You'll Attract Unavailable Men Too

We've talked about ghosters and exters and love bombers and kittenfishers and lions and tigers and bears . . . oh my! It's enough to make a girl stop and ask herself, *Is there something* I *am doing to consistently draw inconsistent men to me like moths to a flame?*

Someone asked me on Twitter recently, "Do you ever wonder why women like us continue to meet and be attracted to emotionally unavailable men?" And I was like, *whoa*. Sometimes you just need to see your own toxic traits in writing to stop and ask yourself, *Why* do *I do that?*

At the end of the day, that's what all the many dating foibles come down to: emotional unavailability. The reason a man ghosts or flakes or Houdinis or goes back to his ex always boils down to the simple fact that he is emotionally unavailable . . . to us, at least.

I have struggled with this issue in my dating life for as long as I can remember. I often feel like catnip for unavailable men: men who are emotionally unavailable, physically unavailable, or, in some really unfortunate cases, both. This can range anywhere from men who are just getting out of serious relationships or coming out of a divorce to men who live across the country. Which begs the questions, am I a magnet for unavailable men, or am I actively *choosing* unavailable men?

When you see a pattern like this repeat itself over and over in your life, it's wise to pause and try to get to the root of the problem. Because it's not usually as simple as being about the thrill of the chase or wanting what you can't have. It's usually about something much deeper . . . something you likely don't want to admit to or about yourself. But the only way to stop making self-defeating choices is to confront your own self-defeating behaviors head on. So let's dive right in, shall we? Why *do* we always seem to turn away the emotionally mature men and yearn for the emotionally stunted ones?

- Fear of commitment. Yes, ladies, it's not just the menfolk. We can be scared of commitment too. Remember the movie *Runaway Bride*? As much as I think I want to settle down and can't wait to be married, the pull of the single life is strong. Especially when you've been single for the majority of your life. We single ladies have complete freedom, march to the beat of our own drummers, and don't answer to anyone. And, yes, singleness can sometimes be lonely and exhausting and challenging . . . but it can also be wild and footloose and fancy-free. I am set in my own ways. The idea of someone coming into my life and changing it all around is a little scary. So I think sometimes I push away the men who I know intuitively would make solid life partners; they represent being tied down, and I gravitate toward the ones I know deep down will never commit. How do you fix this internal glitch, you ask? Well, I'll let you know the formula when I figure it out! But therapy is helping me get to the bottom of my commitment phobia one step at a time and is a huge part of my self-care routine. I highly recommend you incorporate it into yours too.

- We are not emotionally available to ourselves. Meaning, we aren't great about tending to our own emotional needs, so why would we be attracted to men who are? Other people tend to adopt the same attitude about us that *we* have about us . . . and if we neglect ourselves, we will seek out others who neglect us too. That's why self-love is sooooooo important! It sets the tone for our entire lives and especially our love lives. How *you* treat you teaches others how to treat you.
- And finally, lack of self-worth. This goes hand-in-hand with the point above. If we don't believe we are worthy of the very best that love and life have to offer, and if we don't believe we deserve full-on, no-holds-barred, emotionally engaged partners, we will never attract those types of people. We will always settle for the love we *think* we deserve, and if our self-worth tank is empty, the relationships we choose will be just as empty. Here's the thing: *you are worthy of someone who really, really loves you*! You are worthy of someone who shows up for you, physically and emotionally. You are worthy of the best love. Of readily available love. Of unconditional love. Of brave, bold love. But *you* have to believe it to receive it.

I am happy to report that I haven't attracted or been drawn toward an emotionally unavailable man in over two years. Although I have to constantly check myself to make sure I'm interested in someone for the right reasons, I can honestly say being willing to confront my own nonsense has made me far less willing to deal with other people's. And learning how to show up for myself has helped me learn how to better identify people who will show up for me.

I urge you to decide right now to confront *your* junk. There's no time like the present. If you recognize yourself as someone who also draws or is drawn to emotionally unavailable men, decide right now that the buck stops here. Commit to therapy or find a new therapist that better represents who you are today and can help you become the person you want to be tomorrow . . . and do it for yourself, not for anyone else.

Ultimately, like most things in life, attracting the kind of partner you want and deserve starts with you. There is no magic elixir or love potion or self-help book or therapist that can bring you the kind of love that you don't see yourself as worthy of. When *you* show up for you, when *you* honor and respect you, and when *you* love you . . . others will too. It really is as simple as that.

RULE TO Re-meme-ber

Are all men the same, or are all the men you're *choosing* the same? I joke around as much as anyone about how men make me crazy, but the truth is . . . at any moment, we can stop choosing to entertain the ones who make us crazy. We can learn from our mistakes and work on ourselves and reach the place in our lives where we stop attracting the ghosters and the flakes and the players and the emotionally unavailable guys. It's not always the man's fault. Yes, they are responsible for themselves and their bad behavior, but WE are responsible for choosing to stick around after they've shown us those bad behaviors. WE are responsible for the kind of people we allow into our lives. And WE are responsible for raising our standards and making better choices and tending to our own emotional needs so that we stop attracting people who neglect them. That's it. That's the word. Mic drop.

It's not always the man's fault. Yes, they are responsible for themselves and their bad behavior, but WE are responsible for choosing to stick around after they've shown us those bad behaviors.

13

Fact or Fiction?

Are Men Really Ever Intimidated by Women?

Remember Chandler Bing? Not the lovably neurotic and noncommittal character played by Matthew Perry, but the lovably neurotic and noncommittal character from the beginning of the book, who almost pulled a New Year's Eve no-show on me? Let's welcome him back to the program, shall we? Good old Chandler Bing and I have a richly complicated history from which we can learn much, including the answer to that age-old question, "Are men really ever intimidated by women, or is that a line they throw at us to get out of having to admit they're just not that into us?"

Chandler Bing and I met on a dating app a few years ago. We met face-to-face for the first time at a coffee shop, and from the moment he walked in, I could tell he was twitchy and nervous—before he even drank a single drop of coffee. He later told me he was so nervous because he had looked me up and found my credentials and scoped out my social media pages and felt like he was meeting a "celebrity." (Since I've branded myself "The

Single Woman," I can see how it would be a little intimidating to someone coming into the picture who might potentially change my relationship status and my entire online persona.) As the date wore on, however, CB became more and more at ease until, soon enough, we were laughing like old friends. We seemed to click. (The elusive "click"!) Our senses of humor were very similar, we enjoyed doing the same types of things, we made each other laugh—that first coffee date felt like a really promising start.

CB and I went on to date for about a month, and our time together felt like it was sponsored by Hallmark. Because it was around the holidays, we partook in all the fun festive activities together: Christmas tree lighting, ice skating, Christmas shopping, even a holiday-themed pajama party at a local pub. We had a blast every time we were together, we never exchanged so much as a cross word, and—though we hadn't yet had "the talk"—it felt like we were on the fast track to exclusivity. Things seemed close to perfect between us.

Until I found out that CB was juggling me with at least one other woman. He would tell me he was out with friends and he would be out with her, and vice versa. I was understandably hurt . . . not so much because he was dating other people—he had every right to do so—but because he had lied to me about it. If the first few bricks of a new relationship are built on a foundation of dishonesty, it's nearly impossible to construct anything real and lasting. When I confronted CB about his behavior, he gave me this whole speech about how he knew he "could never be enough" for me and how I "needed someone more impressive" and that he was "intimidated by the idea of being in a relationship" with me. Now, this would be a good time to tell you that until CB gets to know someone, he comes across as quiet and introverted. So while I did feel like there was some grain of truth to what he was saying, I also couldn't help but think he was hoodwinking me because he wasn't that into me, was into the other girl a little bit more, or wanted to have an excuse to keep juggling us both.

Ultimately, we parted ways.

Until the following year, when we ran into each other at a Christmas tree lighting, an event we had attended together the year before. Maybe it was the nostalgia, or the romantic Hallmark-esque atmosphere . . . but at any rate, we picked back up seamlessly, almost like no time had ever passed. CB told me he had hoped to run into me, to which I asked, "Why didn't you call or text?" He said he wasn't sure if I wanted to hear from him, so he didn't risk it. Which seemed to lend itself to the idea that perhaps CB was, as he had said, intimidated by me.

We went on to spend the next month or so casually dating, then came the New Year's Eve fiasco when I Lyfted by his house (which lets you know there was clearly no trust there), and not long after, we had what boils down to a repeat of the year before. As they say, doing the same thing over and over again and expecting different results is the definition of insanity.

So, what gives? I wondered. Was I really *that* intimidating? And do men get intimidated by us at all, or is that just an excuse they give us or that we like to tell ourselves because the truth is too painful to admit? I decided to ask around and get advice from some of my most trusted guy friends, as well as from my social media friends, and get to the bottom of this mystery once and for all.

From the time we're little girls, it feels like it's ingrained in our heads that if a guy is mean to us or rejects us or breaks up with us or generally wants nothing to do with us . . . he must be "intimidated" by us. By our smarts, by our success, by our beauty, by our brains, etc., etc. That simply *has* to be the reason they are choosing not to be with us . . . right?

Or is it?

Well, what I have come to believe after sorting through all the feedback I received from men of various ages, races, relationship statuses, and parts of the country is that, yes, men do sometimes get intimidated by women. But it is almost *always* before they meet (like if he sees a beautiful woman across the room and isn't brave enough to go talk to her) or in the early stages of the dating dance rather than later on, and it is almost *never* enough of a factor to keep a man from being with a woman he really likes or wants to pursue. That said, it *can* sometimes stop him from approaching a woman he's interested in if he spots her out in the wild, works with her, etc.—and if he was super intimidated by a woman on the first date, it can also prohibit him from asking her out for a second date.

So, what makes a woman intimidating to a man?

Among the answers I got: if she's super strong, successful, confident, beautiful, smart, accomplished, or all of the above. One man admitted that the "alpha female" (i.e., a woman who possesses all the qualities and traits he had always wished for himself) was intimidating but still inspiring to him . . . which I thought was a wonderfully transparent answer.

Some guys said they don't get intimidated at all. Others said they get intimidated frequently. I think, as with all things, the truth likely lies somewhere in the middle.

Some interesting notes: The general consensus is that dating apps cut down on the intimidation factor; meaning, a man who might be too intimidated to approach a woman he finds attractive at a coffee shop wouldn't have any issue approaching her on a dating app. Dating apps provide a buffer against rejection and require very little risk, as opposed to walking up to a complete stranger at the gym and asking for her digits.

One friend said that if a man is genuinely intimidated by a woman, his ego won't allow him to let on that he's intimidated by her, while another lifelong friend added, "Over the years, guys realized women don't get nearly as upset if the guy says he's 'intimidated' by her as opposed to the other reasons he might have for walking away . . . so guys have adopted that as an excuse. Guys may think a woman is out of their league, certainly, but that's *before* the approach, whether online or in person. A guy might realize after meeting a woman that he can't live up to her standards, but I don't think that means he's 'intimidated.' I think it just means he knows that she's a ten and he's a solid seven. Or she's got it all together and he's still a work in progress."

So what can we deduce from all this informal data? Are men ever intimidated enough by a woman to walk away from her?

Yes—I believe that sometimes a man can be too intimidated by a woman to approach her at all.

Yes—I believe that sometimes, once he does approach her, he might then be too intimidated by her to ask for her number. Or if he does ask for her number, he might be too intimidated to actually *use* it and call or text to ask her out. (This is why there are times we never get that call or text from that man we met out somewhere, whom we seemed to instantly click with, and we are completely baffled by his lack of follow-through.)

Yes—I believe that sometimes a man can be so intimidated by a woman on the first date or two that he feels he could never quite rise to her level, so he fails to pursue her any further.

But no—beyond that, I think the whole intimidation excuse is just that: an excuse.

As my lifelong friend pointed out, a lot of guys have adopted the intimidation excuse as a way to let a woman down easy, because it's the least hurtful way to reject her. In fact, it's almost a compliment. It's hard to be mad at a man who tells you that you're "too amazing" for him to be with, LOL!

Taking all our research into consideration, I think it's safe to say,

I was never getting a ring
from Chandler Bing.
Because Chandler Bing
didn't mean a thing (he said).

Honestly, here's what I believe it all boils down to:

Yes, men can be intimidated by women. Yes, women can be intimidated by men. But ultimately, a relationship both parties genuinely want and are willing to put in the effort and go the distance for will never fail due to intimidation. And most definitely, a long-term relationship will never end due to intimidation. So, if you, like me, were handed that line by someone you had been dating at least semiregularly for any decent amount of time, please know that it was just that: a line. And you've gotta cut that line before you sink like an anchor right along with the relationship. Because any man who truly wants to be with you will find a way. There ain't no mountain high enough or river wide enough to keep him away.

If a man *says* he's not enough for you . . . then he's not enough for you. Believe him. Because what he's really telling you is that he's not willing to do what it takes to *be* enough for you. Don't waste your time trying to convince him otherwise or trying to lessen yourself to make him feel less inadequate. The right one for you will bask in your shine . . . he won't be intimidated by it or try to diminish it.

RULE TO Re-meme-ber

In life, and especially in dating . . . if they wanted to, they would.

If they wanted to call you, they would.

If they wanted to text you, they would.

If they wanted to ask you out, they would.

If they wanted to be your boyfriend, they would.

If they wanted to marry you, they would.

If they wanted to stop seeing other people, stop creeping around behind your back, stop being shady, and generally get their act together so as not to lose you . . . they would.

So please stop buying into the whole "he's too scared, he's too busy, he's too intimidated, he's too shy, he's too much of a friend to risk the friendship, he's too focused on his career, he's too damaged from past relationships, he's too closed off, he's too _____" excuses.

Get honest with yourself. It might be painful, but it is also incredibly freeing. The truth will always set you free. Free to stop wasting time. Free to stop waiting around on him or anyone else to love you. Free to go in search of someone who wants the things you want and, more importantly, wants *you* the same way you want them.

It's so simple.

If they wanted to . . . they would.

That's really all you need to know.

It's so simple.
If they wanted to . . . they would.
That's really all you need to know.

14

I Spy with My Little Eye . . . the Wrong Guy

Clues That a Relationship Might Be Wrong for You

After Chandler Bing and I crashed and burned the second time, it probably would have been a solid idea for me to pause and take a step back from dating for a moment. I say "probably" because, of course, that's not what I did. In my defense, I wasn't actively out there looking to meet someone. Nope, my next "someone" found me, about two months later. On the dance floor. In the form of my twentysomething dance instructor.

I had started taking dance lessons again to kick off the new year, and about two months into my lessons, things with my instructor took a romantic turn. I think the attraction for me to—let's call him Johnny Castle—was twofold: (1) I have a lifelong obsession with dancing and, in particular, the movie *Dirty*

Dancing (yes, I have worked a mention of *Dirty Dancing* into every book I've written). I have taken ballroom dance lessons a few different times over the years. I've competed in a celebrity dance competition in which I danced to—you guessed it—"The Time of My Life." I have even visited the resort where the movie was filmed: Mountain Lake Lodge in Virginia (aka the real Kellerman's). *Dirty Dancing* is pretty much a part of my DNA at this point, so I am a complete sucker for a man who can dance. (2) Johnny Castle was so different from Chandler Bing, or from any guy I had ever dated, and that was really appealing to me.

I tend to be drawn to intense, deeply intellectual, and bookish sorts of guys. Johnny Castle wasn't any of those things. He wasn't overly cerebral, he wasn't in his head all the time, he didn't overthink life, or really anything, as I often did and as a lot of the guys I dated tended to do. He was just happy and goofy and sweet and easy. And because he was still in his twenties, he was insanely energetic and excited and spontaneous and just completely exuberant about life. Rather like a great big excited puppy dog, in the best way. He lived completely in the now, and he made me want to as well. He made me happy. And for a moment, that was enough.

For a moment.

To keep it 100 percent with you guys . . . Johnny Castle was also a bit of a hot mess. He was younger than me, which wouldn't have been a deal breaker in and of itself, but he acted younger than me. But the age factor was only one of our incompatibilities. He never had any money because as soon as he got paid, it would burn a hole in his pocket. He didn't have a car, so at times it was a struggle for us to make plans. He was a smoker, which is a major turnoff to me (sorry, smokers, but it's not cute). And his grammar and spelling skills were, in a nutshell, an affront to the English language. Now I'm not perfect by *any* stretch of the imagination, but I should have realized when I saw his text messages that he was not a good fit for a book lover and professional writer. We're talking *all* the *you're/your* and *their/they're/there* and *to/two/too* errors.

The entire time I was dating Johnny Castle, and it was only for about a month or so, I would ask myself, *Mandy, what are you doing? This guy is not your person.* And inner Mandy would come back with, *Oh, I'm looking at his heart this time . . . not his issues. I'm living in the moment. I'm not overthinking things!* And thus I would continue stubbornly proceeding down the path I was on, determined to turn this pumpkin of a relationship into a big, beautiful horse-drawn carriage.

The human body is an amazing thing. It's constantly sending us clues in the form of pain, sickness, or emotional distress. When we ignore these clues, it will send us another and another and another . . . until we stop stubbornly barreling down the path we're on and pause to ask ourselves what message we need to be receiving. It never ceases to amaze me how life will keep sending us the same tests over and over and over again until we pass them.

As the relationship wore on, my body began to rebel against me. A few days into dating Johnny Castle, I got sick. And I never get sick. Like . . . ever. I mean, I work from home, meaning I basically exist in a germ-free incubator. And even when I don't feel well, I never run a fever. I can't tell you the last time I had a fever. My normal body temperature hovers around 97 degrees. (My mom says I'm a frog.) And yet there I found myself, knee-deep in this relationship that, intuitively, I knew I shouldn't be in, with a crud that wouldn't go away. I was congested, I had an awful, hacking cough, and one night, my temperature spiked to 101.

It was like my body was rejecting the relationship.

That crud hung on for the entire duration of the relationship. I could have bought stock in Halls with the number of cough drops I consumed. And when the relationship ended, I bet you can guess what went with it. Yep! The crud. The sickness went away completely and almost immediately. Now, I'm sure there are naysayers out there who would say the two things aren't related, but our bodies are amazing, miraculous, wondrous machines designed to reject foreign objects (and people) that don't belong there. And we need to trust ourselves and our bodies to do what they were designed to do: protect us from harm. Not just physical harm but emotional harm. That's why it's so vital to listen not just to your gut and your heart but also to your body—on all fronts, whether it's a new diet, a new exercise routine, or a new relationship.

There are other clues you can look for when it comes to determining whether the person you're dating might be wrong for you:

- If all your friends and/or your family dislike or mistrust your new boo . . . chances are, he is not the one for you. The people closest to you, your inner circle, can see things you can't when you're all caught up in your love bubble.
- If your children (or really any children in your life) have an aversion to him . . . that's another clue. Children are so pure and unfiltered, they have an amazing ability to distinguish the real from the fake, the good from the bad. And they have absolutely no fear in telling you about it.
- If your dog who is normally a perfect angel turns into Cujo and goes into attack mode every time your significant other gets within fifty feet . . . *hello!* Another sign. Animals are very sensitive and seem to instinctively know who's trustworthy and who's not.
- Finally, even if your body isn't reacting in a negative way physically, pay attention to your emotions and your gut. If any part of you feels unsettled, even if you can't put your finger on exactly why, that's a huge red flag that you need to heed.

After about a month, I called it quits with Johnny Castle. I wished him the best, and he danced his way and I danced mine. No drama, no strife . . . I handed him a one-way ticket out of my life. Because that's really the only healthy, smart thing you can do once you realize, and are willing to admit, that you've found yourself in the wrong relationship. And I definitely was. Yes, I wanted to find love . . . but I didn't want to lose myself in the process. Every time we compromise, every time we settle, even just a little bit, we lose little pieces of ourselves. And that eventually starts to erode our self-love, our self-worth, and our self-esteem.

Ultimately, only you can decide who stays in your life and who goes. But when your heart is telling you one thing and your gut another . . . follow your nose (instinct). It always knows! (Points if you remember what vintage cereal commercial that's from.)

Our bodies know. Our friends know. Our pets know. Our children know. Our emotions know. And if someone being in your life sets any or all of these things out of order, the simple truth is . . . they don't belong there.

RULE TO

Re-meme-ber

Here's the thing: You could be the most perfect person to ever walk the earth . . . and you still won't fit the bill or check all the boxes for the wrong person. Johnny Castle wasn't a *bad* person; he just wasn't *my* person. And I wasn't his. Sometimes it comes down to the fact that the two of you are not the right fit. Square peg, round hole. Every person until the right person is the wrong person. Instead of being bummed every time the wrong one exits your life . . . celebrate the fact that you're one step closer to the RIGHT one!

Every person until the right person
is the wrong person. Instead of being
bummed every time the wrong one exits
your life . . . celebrate the fact that you're
one step closer to the RIGHT one!

15

It Takes Two to Tango

Learning When to Lead and When to Follow in Love

I like to try to glean the lesson from every situation in my life, especially every dating situation I find myself in. Once things ended with Johnny Castle, I was able to step back and see the bigger picture of what those dance lessons were all about for me. And they weren't about him at all. Nope, I was done letting the swipe rule my life and making everything in life about a guy. This was about me. After all, the whole reason I had gotten back into dance in the first place was because it was part of a New Year's resolution to become a better version of myself.

When I started taking dance again, I set a couple of goals: (1) to learn how to let go with greater grace and (2) to recapture my childlike joy. So when the opportunity arose for me to start taking ballroom dance lessons again, I jumped at the chance. Here was an opportunity to achieve both of my New Year's resolutions plus do something I loved all in one fell swoop!

I've always been a leader. I think a big reason for that is because I've also always been a control freak. I'm terrible at delegation and tend to live by the mindset, "If you want something done right, you have to do it yourself." This way of doing things has typically served me well in my career. Because of my single-minded, determined, independent approach, I literally built a brand from scratch. I created a social media movement that reaches millions of women across the world every day. I've written four books (actually, the one you're reading right now is book five!), including one *New York Times* bestseller. I've worked with Oprah. *Oprah*. I mean, come on . . . that's the Holy Grail! I list all these accomplishments not to humble-brag but to point out how being a leader and hustling and charting my own career path instead of waiting for someone else to blaze a trail for me or show me the way has helped me achieve a body of work beyond my wildest dreams.

But guess what? Being a 24/7 leader and bossbabe and control freak has *not* always served me well in my personal life. Why? Because, spoiler alert (and this is truly shocking): it turns out people in relationships don't like to be controlled. They don't like to be told what to do. Healthy relationships require an equal balance of give and take, lead and follow, push and pull, in order to work.

I first took dance lessons in my twenties and had fallen madly in love with ballroom dance. The classy waltz, the jazzy foxtrot, the spicy tango—I loved every last bit of it. There's a joy and freedom that dancing brings that is simply unparalleled. Since it had been around twelve years since I had danced, I was eager to see what I remembered and if I would slide right back into the groove.

Five minutes into my first lesson, I started to recognize the difference between dancing in my twenties and dancing at age forty. In my twenties, I was still becoming who I was going to be. I was still honing my leadership skills. I wasn't as set in my ways. And at age forty? I had no problem going into any room or any situation and taking control. But guess what? You can't "take control" in ballroom dance. That's not how it works. The gentleman leads, the lady follows . . . and from this synergy, a beautiful dance is born.

The only problem was, I was exerting *way* too much energy and not enough synergy by trying to control the partnership. There were moments when I would push when I was supposed to pull. I would anticipate the wrong move and do the wrong thing. I would try to lead a dance I didn't even know the steps to. And I'm pretty sure I made poor Johnny Castle want to pull his hair out. (Allow me to interject here to say that while JC may have been a Hot Mess Express at dating, he was an absolute whiz on the dance floor, and an excellent teacher.) But my desire for control meant dances that should have been fun and easy and lovely became a struggle. And both JC and I were intensely frustrated.

You can't effectively lead if you are unwilling to effectively follow. It takes humility and openness and even bravery to let go and let yourself be led . . . but it's a necessary part of being a good partner—on the dance floor and in life. I had forgotten that. I had been so busy doing things my way over the past few years, I hadn't stopped to think that sometimes my way isn't the best way. That's a side effect of singleness, I suppose. You become so accustomed to doing almost everything for yourself, you forget how to let anyone help you.

Dancing is very much symbolic of relationships. It's two people working together toward a common goal: a beautiful, effortless dance. If both people are leading at the same time or following at the same time, the dance doesn't work. Or if one person insists on having things their way and isn't open to the other person's point of view, the dance doesn't work. Neither does the relationship.

After a few lessons, I started to let go a little and let myself be led. And slowly, the dance started to flow. As do most things when we learn to release our grip of control and just *trust*.

Trust is hard for me. I tend to be a stage-five clinger, not when it comes to people, but when it comes to life and love in general. I'm terrified to let go and risk losing control. I want to eliminate every single potential risk factor and take away the slightest probability of getting hurt before I make my move. But that's not how love, or life, works. Or dancing, for that matter. You have to be willing to surrender to someone else sometimes, and trust them to take the lead, regardless of whether that someone is your dance partner, a person you're dating, a friend, a family member, a coworker, or even God.

Trust might be hard for you too. In this day and age of being ghosted or flaked on or juggled with five or six different women, trust can feel . . . dangerous. Believe me, I get it. But isn't love, by definition alone, a little dangerous? Throwing your heart out there and hoping it gets caught instead of dropped and broken? Giving another human being that kind of power over you? Trusting that if you take your hands off the reins for a moment and just surrender to the process, you won't veer wildly off course? Love is nothing if not wild and untamed and terrifying and exhilarating and crazy and beautiful, all at the same time. I'd call that the good kind of dangerous, wouldn't you? And the beautiful thing about being a strong, take-charge bossbabe like yourself is that you don't have to be one thing or the other. You don't have to be either sweet or sassy. You don't have to be either strong or vulnerable. And you don't have to be either a leader or a follower. You can be both. You can be all things. And your life, and your relationships, will be better for it.

About a month into my dance lessons, I finally learned how to fully let go and follow someone else's lead. And my dancing became free and joyful and light and fun. I'm still practicing the art of letting go and following someone else's lead in love . . . but I'll get there. Because I want my life and my relationships to be just as free and joyful and light and fun as my dancing.

I want to encourage you to let go a little too. Stop pacing, stop sweating, stop controlling, stop fretting. Stop trying to cling and grasp and control the outcome. Stop refusing to allow yourself to feel because you're afraid you might get hurt. Some of the most beautiful things, beautiful dances, and beautiful relationships happen when we just . . . let . . . go.

RULE TO

Re-meme-ber

Just as leaves on trees dance and twirl and fall gently to the ground in autumn, returning come spring, you can let go of everything you're clinging so hard to and trust that if it's meant for you—*truly* meant for you—it will stick. Or it will return when it's supposed to. Or it will go away and never come back, and you know what? You'll be okay. I promise. I know now that the people and relationships and opportunities meant for me don't have to be forced, they don't have to be chased, they don't have to be clung to. And they don't have to be constantly bossed around or controlled either. If I have to do any of those things to get something or to keep it in my life, I don't want it. It's okay to let go a little. It's actually imperative to the success of your relationships that you do. You can relax and surrender and trust someone else to lead sometimes. Because the only people who will leave your life when you let go are the ones who aren't meant to be there anyway.

You can relax and surrender and trust someone else to lead sometimes. Because the only people who will leave your life when you let go are the ones who aren't meant to be there anyway.

16

My Breakup with Dating

Why I Gave Dating a Swipe Left and Swiped Right on Myself

After my latest relationship crash and burn (or emergency landing and smolder, as the case may be), I was kind of just . . . over dating. I felt completely deflated. Although Johnny Castle and I didn't have a big dramatic ending or heart-wrenching breakup, I had just come off two failed dating attempts back-to-back, and that can really take it out of a girl. And even though my New Year's Eve Lyft fiasco had shaken me out of complacency and inspired me to take back control of my dating life, I knew that in order to move forward and date in a positive and healthy way, I needed to pause, reflect, and take inventory of my dating life so I could figure out where the disconnect was between where I had been and where I wanted to go. Sometimes, like our computers, our love lives need to be completely unplugged for a minute so they can breathe and reboot.

I was forty years old and had never been married, never been engaged, and never really even come close to either. I had just had one relationship fall apart with a guy I had met organically and another one fall apart with a guy I had met on a dating app—so the argument could be made that neither approach seemed to be working for me. Since I doubted my dream man was going to be magically beamed down into my apartment while I was binge-watching *The Golden Girls*, I started to feel like I was running out of options.

When I gazed at the past twenty-five years of ex-files, I started to find myself feeling very much like Charlotte from that episode of *Sex and the City* when she famously proclaims, "I've been dating since I was fifteen! I'm exhausted! Where is he?!"

Where is he? He's not at church, I had discovered. He definitely wasn't at the bar. I hadn't found him online. He wasn't the responsible, gainfully employed forty-eight-year-old I had a brief crush on a few months prior or the irresponsible twenty-seven-year-old with major Peter Pan syndrome I had just spent a month trying to help get his life on track. (I'm a fixer . . . what can I say?) He wasn't any of my exes, on whom I had spent exhaustive amounts of time and research, recycling several times just to make sure. So where *was* he?! I had not the foggiest idea.

As I contemplated my recent dating experiences, I started to realize that over the past few years, as I'd grown increasingly frustrated with dating in general, I had lowered my standards for the people I was welcoming into my life. Instead of taking the time to pause and really consider if every guy I met and had a connection with was a good fit for my life . . . or even slowly easing into the relationship to make sure it was the right one for me . . . I had been guilty of jumping in with both feet. It was like, "Oh, okay. You're cute. You're single. We seem to click. Let's just skip right over 'dating' to 'boyfriend and girlfriend,' and start spending every waking moment together until both of us have given up everything else in our lives except each other!"

And I had the audacity to wonder why it had never worked out.

With Johnny Castle in particular, I realized . . . I hadn't even actively *chosen* him. I had more just sort of *settled* for him because he happened to be a cute guy who was just . . . *there.* I wasn't a girl, standing in front of a boy, asking him to love her. I was a girl, standing in front of a boy, asking him to hang out with her and entertain her and keep her from being bored. At what point had I stopped choosing my love life and started settling for it?

I decided right then and there, *no more.* I told myself, "This unhealthy cycle of getting into a relationship with whomever happens to be standing in front of me and paying me attention stops right now!" It was fruitless and endlessly frustrating and had brought me nothing but multiple heartbreaks . . . sometimes over the same guy. Just because I wanted to be married and have a family didn't mean I had to try to magically transform every guy who happened to show me a little attention into a serious love interest.

I knew what I had to do. I had to break up with . . . dating.

A week or so after things ended with Johnny Castle, I went on a carpe diem road trip to the beach with some girlfriends. It was a spontaneous adventure, the kind I love best, that gave me a much-needed time-out from regular everyday life and the chance to think about my many dating crashes and burns over the past couple of years. At some point during the weekend, I decided I was officially stepping off the relationship roller coaster and taking a break, a pause, a beat, a time-out, a hiatus . . . a sabbatical from settling, if you will . . . which was something I had been doing a lot as of late: just settling for whoever happened to show up in my life instead of taking the time to evaluate if they actually belonged there. I marked this monumental decision with a message in a bottle . . . the gist of which was that I was releasing my love life and my desire to be married someday into the hands of my Higher Power, and I was releasing control. Something I don't tend to be great at. It was a true "Jesus, take the wheel" moment, and as I tossed the glass bottle into the ocean, I threw my hands up in the air and surrendered my path, my process, and my romantic destiny . . . completely. My recent ballroom dance experience, along with my failed relationship with my ballroom dance instructor, had taught me that I couldn't keep clinging to, controlling, and trying to force and manipulate inappropriate and ill-fitting romantic prospects into the man of my dreams. It was time to get back in touch with *me* and what I really wanted out of love. It was time to recalibrate and reevaluate, and to refine and raise my standards.

It was time to just be me, Mandy, for a while, without anyone else. It was time to stand alone. It was time to trust that God had my back and that the people who were meant to be in my life would find their way there without me nudging them along. Because if I had to force it or settle for it . . . it wasn't meant for me in the first place. And it was also time, once and for all, to let the ones who were not meant for me go. Like, let really, really *go*. I knew I had to stop recycling my exes, stop leaving the door open for ghosts of relationships past to float in and out of my life, stop giving people who had already hurt me once chance after chance after chance to do it again. It was time to just *stop*.

So I did. I gave dating a swipe left, and I swiped right on myself . . . and I had arguably the best summer of my entire life.

I chased waterfalls and kayaked rivers, I hiked trails and did yoga with goats, I made new friends and traveled winding country roads, I pushed myself outside my comfort zone in a million different ways, and I truly, truly lived my best life. I wasn't the slightest bit concerned about dating or finding love . . . and a beautiful thing happened when I stopped that endless search. I found *myself* and reclaimed pieces of myself I had lost along the way—pieces that had been chipped away over the past few years by every heartbreak, by every time I was ghosted or disappointed or disheartened by love. One of the most beautiful realizations for me was learning that sometimes the quickest way to find your way out of an emotional or metaphorical or even relational wilderness is to go wander around in the *actual* wilderness for a while. With every step I took that summer, another piece of my heart came back. Another giggle came back. Another little sparkle in my eye came back. The parts of myself that I had lost to dating had beautifully, wonderfully returned . . . and I knew that when I was ready to press the start button on my love life again, I would be approaching it with a completely different perspective. I wouldn't be looking for "my person" because I had realized that *I* am my person. I was all I ever really needed all along. Just call me Dorothy Gale from Kansas, because I had remembered that the power was already in *me* to embrace and celebrate and love my life. I didn't need a man to do any of those things for me. Certainly, finding love would be completely amazing and was still very much in my plan . . . but I had stopped looking for anyone to bring me anything or give me anything or add anything whatsoever to my life except the pleasure of their company, because I had finally learned that I didn't need anyone to complete me. I completed me.

It was truly my #HealingGirlSummer.

My dating break would go on to last six months. And it was one of the best, most empowering experiences of my life. I would eventually return to the dating game, and I would be almost immediately faced with the inevitable disappointments . . . but they wouldn't shake me or break me like they had before. My feet were firmly planted in who I was.

That's what my breakup with dating did for me.

So how do you know if *you* need your own dating vacay? Here are a few hints that it might be time to give dating a swipe left so you can swipe right on yourself:

- You're currently dating not because you genuinely want to be dating but because you are frantically trying to avoid being alone. If this is the case, it's definitely time to step away from the dating app. A healthy relationship will never be an "escape." And a happy, healthy, full life will never need to be escaped *from*.

- You rushed into a new relationship way too soon after your last one ended. You can't expect the new person to be a Band-Aid for what the last person did. When you start a new relationship before taking time to heal from the last one, you are dragging the past and all its heartache and wounds and trauma into the present. It's so important to take a pause after every relationship in order to give yourself time to properly grieve it and then leave it. Otherwise you'll remain hurt and broken and keep attracting even more of that hurt and brokenness into your life. Ain't nobody got time for that!
- You consistently pick the same kinds of romantic partners over and over again (i.e., the *wrong* ones). The only way to break that cycle is to break up with dating for a season and spend some time doing the hard work on yourself so you can figure out *why* you are attracted to people who aren't good for you, and then take the necessary steps to change. (Believe me, as someone who has done and will continue to do the therapy and the hard work on myself—confronting yourself is the most challenging and most rewarding thing you will ever do.)
- You've recently found yourself with the mentality, "It's better to have anyone than no one." Ummmm . . . *no*. It's better to have *no one* than the wrong *someone*. And I don't know about you, but when it comes to picking the person I want to share my life with, I don't want just "anyone."
- You're just generally burned out with dating. Part of self-care is recognizing when something is causing you more

> pain and tears than smiles and cheers. Dating comes with its inevitable ups and downs, but if you've been in the valley so long you can't even see the mountaintop, it's time to tell dating to take a hike and reclaim your life. When I've struggled with how to finish a chapter of this book, I've closed my laptop and walked away for a little while. Sometimes even for the rest of the night. And when I come back, I always feel refreshed, recharged, and ready to go. The same goes for dating. We need to give ourselves permission to lay it down, go about our lives, and only pick it back up when we are good and ready. There is no race. There is no rush. Dating will be here when you get back. And it will most likely look a whole lot sunnier and more hopeful with fresh eyes and a renewed spirit.

I want to encourage you to take your own dating pause if you've been feeling frustrated or disheartened with your dating life as of late. It can be a few days or a few weeks or a few months. It's entirely up to you. I didn't set a specific time frame; I just followed where my gut led. I can honestly say that my six-month dating break was one of the best decisions I ever made. Breaks and breathers from dating to tend to you and your healing and your growth and your restoration are healthy and necessary. Not everyone deserves a seat at your table . . . and sometimes we need seasons of eating alone to remind us of that.

RULE TO Re-meme-ber

Until you heal, until you do the hard work on *you*, until you spend time alone and confront your own baggage and dig deep and learn how to love yourself . . . really love yourself, not just in words but in action . . . you are not ready for love.

Why? Because you can only attract what you already are. And if you're broken and hurting and rushing from relationship to relationship and are completely emotionally unavailable to yourself, then that's exactly who and what you will attract. YOU CAN ONLY ATTRACT WHAT YOU ALREADY ARE. And until you are a whole and complete person on your own, you will never attract another whole and complete person. And relationships will continue to be Band-Aids and not blessings. So stop. Take a step back. Pause the frantic search for love and instead search for *you*. Search for self-love. Search for wholeness and healing. And then you won't have to seek after healthy love because *it* will find *you*.

YOU CAN ONLY ATTRACT WHAT YOU ALREADY ARE.
And until you are a whole and complete person on your own, you will never attract another whole and complete person.

17

There Are No Second Chances in Love

Why You Should Steer Clear of Relationship Reboots

Back in my day, when a beloved television show ended, we the audience would collectively weep and wail and gnash our teeth as we bid farewell to the characters we had grown to know and love for however many seasons. And this was back in the stone age before Netflix or Hulu (or even TBS), so you had no guarantee you would ever see those characters again. When *Dawson's Creek* ended, it was an *event*. I took off work the next day, listened to "I Don't Want to Wait" by Paula Cole on repeat, and ate my weight in Chunky Monkey as I mourned the end of an era.

Now when a show ends, you turn off your TV, go about your life, and wait a few years for the reboot. (Or in *American Idol's* case, you wait about five minutes.)

Over the past few years, along with *American Idol*, we've seen reboots of dozens of classic (and some not-so-classic) TV shows like *Will & Grace*, *Full House*, *Roseanne*, *Gilmore Girls*, *Murphy Brown*, *Charmed*, *Veronica Mars*, and *Party of Five*—just to name a few. (Time out: A *Saved by the Bell* reboot is also now canon, and I gotta say, I'm pretty stoked about that one. Time back in.) Hollywood either has a case of serious nostalgia or has simply run out of new material. (Which, coincidentally, is also why we attempt to reboot relationships. We'll get to that.) The list of movies that have been or are currently in the process of being rebooted is even longer than the one of repurposed TV shows: *Charlie's Angels*, *Footloose*, *Ghostbusters*, *A Star Is Born*, pretty much every beloved Disney film, *Jumanji*, *Top Gun*, *Halloween* . . . and on and on and on. We've got reboots for *days*.

I can't lie, y'all . . . I've always been a sucker for a good second-chance story. On the small screen and the big screen (and also in my love life but again, we're getting to that). I'm a total TV nerd and movie buff (as you can probably tell by the fact that I've renamed my exes in this book after TV or movie characters), and sometimes it can be hard for me to draw the line between what I *think* love is supposed to be like, according to my favorite shows and films, and the reality of what love is *actually* like.

I mean, who doesn't love a good rom-com starring the lovable cad of a boyfriend who lets his awesome (and, of course, perfect, gorgeous, and flawlessly thigh-gapped) girlfriend down in new appalling ways every single day, who probably doesn't have a job, goals, ambition, or the ability to stay faithful for longer than one episode of a Netflix binge, and who doesn't realize the error of his ways until said girlfriend has left him high and dry and taken her Netflix password with her? (Or basically, Matthew McConaughey in every romantic comedy he's ever been in.) We all know what happens next, right? Mr. McConaughey sees the light, chases his leading lady to the airport/train station/boat dock/Hertz Rent-A-Car, etc., miraculously becomes a better man than he was five minutes earlier, and professes his undying love. Then she takes him back, no questions asked. They kiss, we swoon, the credits roll. And, once again, Hollywood succeeds in making us forget why exes are in fact . . . exes. (That said, I'd be the first one in line at a *How to Lose a Guy in 10 Days* sequel, reboot, remake, *whatever.*)

And who doesn't also love seeing TV characters you haven't seen in a few years back on your screen and learning where their lives have taken them since you parted ways? The nostalgia is real, y'all. So real that we completely forget about the played-out storylines and tired writing that led the show to go away in the first place. So real that we welcome them back with open arms, despite the fact that we were *this close* to kicking them to the curb when the show got canceled before we could do so. So real that we only remember the good, happy, and misty watercolored memories of the way we were and conveniently forget all the bad, sad, and tearstained misery of the way we would still be had we not been rescued from wasting more years of our lives on a TV show that was never good for us in the first place.

Any of this ring a bell with anyone?

There are certain ex-boyfriends out there who will always come back around. Who will always find a way to reboot themselves no matter how long they've been gone. Who, like Michael Myers in the 437 *Halloween* movies and sequels and reboots, never really die. No matter how bad the breakup was or what remote, deserted island you move to in order to escape him—he will find you. He will online stalk his way back into your life via a tweet, a snap, a Facebook friend request, or an Instagram DM. He might even start a new account to get to you since you blocked him on all the old ones. And more than likely it will happen right at the very second that you *finally* get over him. It's like there's a weird male antenna that receives a signal that you're not hung up on him anymore and his fingers are suddenly drawn to his phone like a moth to a flame. "She's not crying into her pillow every night anymore. I better text her and remind her why she was crying in the first place!"

Yes, some exes will keep coming back and trying to reboot the relationship as long as you'll allow them to. But the problem is, the reasons the relationship ended didn't just magically get resolved during the hiatus. They will still very much be there when the two of you attempt to come back together. And, much like Michael Myers, they will usually be even bigger and badder in the sequel.

While not all exes have bad intentions, it's best to avoid that danger zone like you would a coffee shop with no WiFi or a film with a 27 percent ranking on Rotten Tomatoes. Why? Because as the old adage says, "A leopard never changes its spots." In this case—the spots are whatever reasons you had for ending the relationship in the first place.

Things ended for a reason. Remember that reason. That's something my therapist likes to remind me of every time I come to her about an ex who has popped back up in my life like a game of Whac-A-Mole (or Whac-A-Leopard, I guess).

Whatever spots your particular leopard had when last you saw him, you can bet they're still there—even if he's cleverly hiding them behind a more mature age, smoother talk, or sudden eagerness to commit.

I once tried to date a guy when I was in my early twenties, then again when I was in my midtwenties, then again when I was in my early thirties, and I can categorically say—the third time was *not* the charm. Nope, he was sketchier and shadier every time I gave him another chance. It's like this guy went out of his way to get in his lifetime quota of weird dating behaviors with me. But I just seem to have this soft spot for my exes and wanted to believe, each time he came back, that he had changed. (Spoiler alert: he hadn't.)

Remember Ghostface from chapter 10? I tried to give *him* a second chance and he double-ghosted me in the stand-up heard round the world! And Chandler Bing? My attempt at a relationship reboot with him was like the movie *Groundhog Day*. We literally repeated our exact relationship one year after it ended the first time, complete with him sneaking around behind my back with another woman and lying to me about it.

And who can forget Mr. E, my most infamous ex ever? I attempted to repurpose him time and time again, and every time, the relationship only failed harder and harder. He was truly my "real-life Mr. Big." Except, thankfully, instead of ultimately walking down the aisle with him like Carrie did with Big, I walked away into the sunset, by myself. (By the way, has anyone else, as you have gotten older, thought Carrie should have totally told Mr. Big to go jump in a lake at the end and chosen herself instead? Or picked Aidan when she had the chance? It's funny how romantic the torture of unrequited love can seem when you're younger . . . and yet it completely loses its luster as you get older and just want someone who provides a safe place for you to land.)

I can't help but wonder . . . is this just me? Or is everyone more susceptible to catching feelings for someone they've once had feelings for? Here are some of the reasons I have justified rebooting a relationship:

- I've told myself, "He's changed. He's older and wiser now."
- I've thought to myself, *Things were left unfinished between us, and this is our chance to get it right this time.*
- I've questioned whether he was always the one I was supposed to be with all along and it just took time for us both to realize it, and this was fate bringing us back together.
- I've had selective memory and only remembered the good parts of the relationship and none of the bad.
- I've confused nostalgia for the past with feelings in the present. Being with an ex is comfortable and familiar and

> you don't have to put yourself through the whole process of getting to know someone all over again, and that can be very appealing. (But it's just a mirage.)

Here's the thing: people rarely change *that* much. Now don't get me wrong. I'm not saying people aren't capable of change. I believe they are. I've changed greatly over the past few years. But I got here through intensive struggle and therapy and confronting my own junk. A lot of people aren't willing or able to take the necessary steps to effect real change. Barring a miracle or a massive life overhaul, your ex is still the same guy who told you that you were the love of his life, then broke up with you via text message.

As for the "unfinished business" excuse? I would argue that any ending, no matter how it comes about, is closure. It's okay and even healthy to let some things end messily and badly. You can't put a cherry on top of every sundae. Sometimes things end because they're supposed to end, and you don't get an explanation or an apology or closure. My therapist also likes to remind me that we are responsible for our own closure. You should never leave your peace of mind or ability to move on in someone else's hands.

And finally . . . real love isn't like a movie or a TV show, and it's not supposed to be. Real love doesn't have to chase you to the airport at the end of the movie, because real love doesn't leave in the first place. If he was and is the one you were meant to be with, he would have stuck around. Or you would have stuck around. You both would have stuck around—for the hard stuff, for the intense stuff, for the messy stuff. Don't get so sucked into the idea of a perfect Hollywood ending that you mistake glitter for gold.

Exes are, by definition, bad news. *Exile*, *excommunicate*, *exclude*, *extradite*, *exhume*, *exhausted* . . . do any of these words give you a warm and fuzzy feeling? There's a reason that *ex* comes before *boyfriend*—so it's best to leave that relationship on the cutting room floor and not to try to reboot a moment that probably wasn't all that great to begin with. Besides, when you fill up your DVR with *The X-Files*, you leave no room for *A Current Affair* (wink wink). So the only "ex" you should be engaging is the Exit button on your remote control, and quickly!

Yes, I know some of you are thinking it: sometimes a second chance love story *does* work. Sometimes. But, like the title of one of my favorite vintage scary movies (which also birthed a few pretty terrible sequels), that phenomenon tends to be more of an urban legend than an actual reality. There is always a slim chance when you attempt to reboot a relationship that the two of you will be able to make it work the second time around. But there's a much bigger chance that you'll end up just as hurt and heartbroken and alone as you were the first time around. Remember the truly heinous made-for-TV *Dirty Dancing* reboot? Everybody wanted to put Baby in a corner. That's exactly how most relationship reboots turn out, and is that what you want your love life to be? A live-action #PinterestFail?

Some TV and movie reboots are great . . . but most are not so great and feel like an attempt to recreate magic that fizzled out a long time ago. If you keep revisiting the past and everything that has come before, you'll completely miss out on the future and everything (and everyone!) it has in store. As they say (ironically) in the movie *Scream 2*, "Sequels are, by definition alone, inferior films." And rebooted relationships or relationship sequels are, by definition alone, inferior relationships. So how about we pop open a box of Junior Mints and let the credits roll on what was? There's so much excitement and hope and possibility in the coming attractions of what can still be.

RULE TO Re-meme-ber

Girl, that ex will keep popping up, resurrecting himself, creeping into your inbox with his "WYD" foolishness and generally trying to reboot the relationship as long as you will let him. He will keep you on his hook as long as you'll stay there. He will do the bare minimum to string you along as long as you are content to be strung along. And he will keep treating you like the best friend when you are *clearly* a leading lady (see *The Holiday*—like, see it again and again and again because it's brilliant). But here's the thing: he hasn't changed and neither has the relationship. All he's gonna do is keep wasting your time and stealing your opportunities to meet someone who wants to be with *you* instead of someone who just doesn't want to be alone. But guess what? To paraphrase the original bossbabe, Glinda the Good Witch, *you hold the power, my dear*. You always did. You just had to realize it for yourself. Stop picking up. Stop responding. Leave him on read. Better yet . . . block him and move on with your life. Stop being accessible to people who aren't worthy of your time and certainly not your tears. Let your boundaries, standards, and self-love be like that soaring music they play at the Oscars whenever someone's speech goes too long and shut down *any* thought of rebooting a relationship that was already canceled.

Stop picking up. Stop responding. Leave him on read. Better yet . . . block him and move on with your life. Stop being accessible to people who aren't worthy of your time and certainly not your tears.

18

When Harry Met Sally

Can Men and Women Ever Really Be "Just Friends"?

While we're on the subject of all things movies (and exes), it feels like a perfect time to talk about one of my favorite films of all time, *When Harry Met Sally.*

Premiering in 1989 (the year Taylor Swift was born and also probably way before some of you were) and starring Meg Ryan and Billy Crystal, the classic rom-com explores many hot-button relationship topics of the era and, when rewatched today, surprisingly holds up. That's the thing about love: it's the same yesterday, today, and forever.

Certainly, dating dynamics have changed since then . . . but the primary question the movie explores remains incredibly relevant and is perhaps just as debatable now as it was then.

Can men and women ever be "just friends"?

Let's see what the movie has to say about that.

Harry: Would you like to have dinner? . . . Just friends.

Sally: I thought you didn't believe men and women could be friends.

Harry: When did I say that?

Sally: On the ride to New York.

Harry: No, no, no, no, I never said that. Yes, that's right, they can't be friends . . . unless both of them are involved with other people. Then they can. This is an amendment to the earlier rule. If the two people are in relationships, the pressure of possible involvement is lifted. That doesn't work either. Because what happens then is the person you're involved with can't understand why you need to be friends with the person you're just friends with, like it means something is missing from the relationship and you wanted to go outside to get it. Then, when you say, "No, no, no, no, it's not true, nothing is missing from the relationship," the person you're involved with then accuses you of being secretly attracted to the person you're just friends with, which you probably are—I mean, come on, who are we kidding, let's face it—which brings us back to the earlier rule before the amendment, which is men and women can't be friends. So, where does it leave us?

Sally: Goodbye, Harry.*

As evidenced by the conversation above, the movie starts off with the premise that men and women *can't* be just friends. But then, years later, Harry and Sally cross paths again and actually become friends. And then, years after that, they fall in love. Which brings us back to the original point: Were they ever really "just friends" if they always had the capacity to fall in love?

I'm not sure about Harry and Sally, but in my humble opinion, *yes* . . . men and women can be just friends. How do I know this? Because I have several great male friends. I have these friendships because I added a goal to my vision board this year to nurture the male friendships I already have and to cultivate new ones. The key is this: the health of your friendships, including

* *When Harry Met Sally*, directed by Rob Reiner (Burbank, CA: Warner Bros., 1989).

the ones with guys, depends on the health of *you*. It begins and ends with you. And for perhaps the first time in my life, I feel like I am at a healthy place on all levels: physically, spiritually, emotionally, and mentally. And that has made all the difference. You can't have healthy relationships with other people until you master a healthy relationship with yourself. Throughout my life, I've struggled to achieve and maintain friendships with men because I didn't have good, healthy boundaries in place. Nor was I a very good friend to myself for a long time. And healthy has to happen on the inside before it shows up on the outside.

That said . . . there are some caveats when it comes to men and women being just friends:

1. All my close male friends are single. This is not by coincidence. That isn't to say that married men and women can't have friends of the opposite sex, but in my experience, it can be challenging to respectfully maintain a close friendship with a married person without making their spouse uncomfortable. No friendship is worth putting strain on your friend's marriage. One of my best male friends is married, but he lives across the country now, meaning we only occasionally talk and text. If we were still living in the same city, I doubt we would hang out all the time. It wouldn't make sense for either of us. I can love him and be there for him from a distance, but to try to insert myself into his day-to-day life when he's busy with his wife and daughter simply isn't feasible or appropriate.
2. *Unless* . . . you are in a relationship too. Then the Harry-and-Sally rule from above comes into play. If you are both involved with other people, it tends to lift any awkwardness and potential that the two of you would become romantically involved with each other. Plus, it's fun to have another couple to double-date with!

3. A few of my male friends are lifelong friends, which helps dilute any concern of ever becoming attracted to one another. If you've been friends since kindergarten and you've never developed a crush on each other, it's probably not gonna happen now. I joke that my lifelong guy friends might as well be potted plants to me at this point. Which is not to take away from their amazing qualities, because they are some seriously great catches. But once you've seen someone eat paste, wet their pants, and wallow in the dirt on the playground, you're probably not going to fall head over heels for them—ha! There's just not a lot of mystery or chemistry with someone who feels like your brother.
4. Can you be friends with an ex? I used to think the answer to this was a resounding *no*. Then I switched to Team Yes. But then I tried to strike up a friendship—just a friendship—with Chandler Bing a few months after our second failed attempt at a relationship reboot. And for a little while, it was great. We have a lot in common and enjoy the same types of outdoor activities. We had a blast together that summer, in a completely platonic way. But when a romantic relationship hasn't been over for very long, and the feelings are still somewhat fresh, like cream, they have a way of rising to the top. And that's what happened with us. Things got confusing again, and I ended the friendship. Not all exes are meant to be friends, as there are still intense feelings involved and it's not healthy to try to navigate a friendship with someone you're still very much emotionally entangled with. That said, I *do* think there are instances when it is possible to be friends with an ex. Take a high school sweetheart, for example. We dated for several years and have been friends (almost) ever since. He's like family to me now. Why did this friendship work? After we broke up, we went our separate

ways for a few years, and we both had time to heal and move on with our lives before we came back together as friends. Time, as they say, really does heal all. So yes, some exes can be successful at friendship; however, you have to have really solid boundaries in place and stick to them. When you know in your heart that any ship for a potential romance with that person has sailed, it makes it much easier to navigate the waters of friendship.

5. Never try to use the whole "let's just be friends" thing with someone you still carry a torch for to keep them in your life. If you wouldn't be okay with them coming to you for relationship advice, that's a pretty clear sign that you have no business trying to be their friend. That was one of the big red flags that popped up in my friendship with Chandler Bing. I asked him for advice about another guy one night, and he got all twitchy and agitated before storming out of my house. It was clear that there was something deeper than friendship between us if I couldn't mention another guy's name. Only go down the path of friendship with someone you are legitimately prepared to be *just friends* with, and nothing more. Otherwise, you're just asking for unnecessary heartache. Eventually, that "friend" is going to get involved with someone else romantically, and can your heart really handle a front-row seat to that?

Men and women *can* be just friends . . . but the health of the friendship is always going to depend on the health of the two parties involved. So, as with anything else in life, focus on taking care of you first, and everything else will fall into place. A famous line in another popular film from the Harry-and-Sally era is "If you build it, they will come." If you build a healthy *you*, healthy friendships will come too. Of both the male and female persuasion.

RULE TO Re-meme-ber

The key to successful friendships with men *or* women, as with most things in life, is having healthy boundaries. You have to know where you end, where the other person begins, and what lines are appropriate to cross and not cross. You must always be respectful of that, regardless of whether the other person is male or female, married or single, ex or not. There are few hard and fast rules to anything in life, especially friendship and love. We're all kinda making it up as we go along. But if you do the work on yourself—if you learn to love yourself and look out for yourself and have your own back and set firm, solid, healthy boundaries in your own life—that energy will extend to all your friendships. A beautiful thing has happened in my life the more I've come to know and honor myself: those who didn't know and honor me or didn't want to know and honor me have been naturally weeded out of my life. The chaff is gone and only the wheat remains. That would have never happened if I hadn't been willing to dig deep, pull out some unhealthy mindsets and habits that had taken root, and replace them with healthy seeds of self-love and self-respect and self-worth. All that to say, become your own best friend. Complete yourself. Validate yourself. Love yourself. Then you won't be looking to any of your friendships, male or female, to fill those voids for you. And all your relationships will be a lot better for it.

Become your own best friend. Complete yourself. Validate yourself. Love yourself. Then you won't be looking to any of your friendships, male or female, to fill those voids for you.

19

The Truth about Singleness

Three Lies We Single People Need to Stop Telling Ourselves

Listen. We've been together on this journey for a little while now, so I feel like I can keep it extra real with you about something. Here goes.

Sometimes singleness really sucks.

I know you know this. I know you know that I know you know this. But I feel like I needed to let you know that it's okay to say it out loud sometimes. Or to even scream or shout it out loud if you need to.

One of my favorite things to do on a pretty day is to go read in the park. I have a favorite giant old oak tree that I sit under, and that, coupled with a blanket, a stack of books, and my Starbucks Caramel Frappuccino, makes for a dream day for me. In those quiet, peaceful moments (and sometimes hours) that I sit under that tree in the sunshine, I feel complete and total bliss. It's like the rest of the world fades away and I am free from the busyness of my schedule and email inbox and responsibilities. Free to daydream and travel to faraway magical places in whatever book I'm reading and escape reality for the wild, limitless landscape of my imagination.

One recent day under my tree, however, I happened to look over to my right to a cluster of trees a little deeper into the park. I noticed a hammock tied between two of the trees and smiled, thinking to myself how wonderfully peaceful it looked. Then I looked a little closer and saw that there was a couple lying in the hammock. They had their heads and feet in opposite directions, and each was reading their own book as the hammock lightly rocked back and forth in the breeze. As I watched, I saw the guy reach out and take his girlfriend's (wife's?) hand gently as they both continued to read. It was such a natural, sweet, fluid gesture, something they no doubt did several times every day. To them, it was likely just something they took for granted—reaching out for a hand to grab and finding it. But to me, I might as well have been watching a movie with French subtitles; that's how incomprehensible the certainty of having a hand to hold felt. And in that moment, my heart broke a little.

Though I turned back to my book and stopped staring at the couple—lest they think I was some weird stalker girl—I couldn't shake the feeling of emptiness in my gut. For me, the grand moments of life don't really faze me as a single person: attending my book launches alone, going to the movies alone, not having a date to a friend's wedding. I rarely bat an eye at any of those things and am, for the most part, content and confident to fly solo. It's in the quiet moments that I really feel my aloneness: when someone hurts my feelings and I wish I had someone there to defend me or simply provide a shoulder to cry on, if my GPS takes me somewhere crazy and I have no one to weigh in on which way to go (on the road or in life!), or when I'm sitting under a tree in a park reading a book and wishing I had someone beside me to take my hand the way the guy in the hammock took his lady's hand. In those moments, my walls come down and I admit to myself that sometimes being single just *hurts.*

That feeling usually passes pretty quickly and I remember why I love my singleness so much. The thing I try to remember in those vulnerable moments is this: I don't know whether I'll ever have someone there to grab my hand in the park, but I can't let that stop me from reaching out my hand to grab on to other things. There's so much joy and possibility and life to grab on to that has nothing whatsoever to do with finding love or romance. I can grab my friends' hands. I can grab my nieces' hands. I can grab the opportunity to speak life and hope and love into the hearts of others. I can even grab a pair of designer shoes if I want, because I have no one to answer to about how ridiculously expensive they are! And I can grab happiness. It's there. It's a different sort of happiness than the couple in the hammock—but happiness is still happiness, any way you slice it.

So, having made peace with the fact that singleness sometimes sucks and allowing that to coexist with the fact that I've carved out my little corner of happiness right here in the midst of it, when someone asked me the other day what I think are the biggest challenges single people face, I knew my answer immediately: the lies we tell ourselves. And yes, I'm talking to myself here too, and the lies I allowed myself to believe that day at the park as I watched the happy couple. *There's something wrong with me. I'm irrevocably broken. I'll be alone forever.* That constant broken record that, if we're not careful, can play on repeat in our minds all day long as we search for a logical explanation for our seemingly endless singleness.

Here are three lies we single people need to stop telling ourselves . . . because these false beliefs are particularly hurtful and damaging to our spirits, peace of mind, and self-esteem:

1. **There's something wrong with us because we're single.** There's nothing wrong with us because we are single.

There's no deep explanation here or hidden secret. We're not concealing a hump on our backs or cloven hooves or a third eye. (Okay, well, hopefully we're not. But even if we are, dang it, we're still worthy of love!) Singleness is not a curse thrust upon us. It's not something to be ashamed of. It's not an insult or a weapon to be hurled at us, as our society unfortunately often does, particularly when it comes to social media. You wouldn't believe how many times people have disagreed with something I've tweeted or posted and have retaliated with "Oh, so THAT'S why you're still single!" in an effort to hurt me by using the area of my life in which they think I am the most vulnerable. And, you know what? Singleness *is* an area of my life where I am vulnerable, because I don't understand it. Not being coupled up at age forty-one makes no sense to me, and sometimes it causes me great distress and worry and anxiety to consider the fact that I might never be coupled up. But . . . not being coupled up doesn't mean that I am lacking or deficient or romantically challenged. It simply means that I haven't found the right person (or my "lobster," as Phoebe Buffay would say). We have to stop blaming ourselves and carrying around the weight of feeling broken and screwed up simply because we haven't yet found love. It's simply not true. Certainly, we all have room for growth and are all flawed and imperfect in our own unique ways, but that is true for everyone who walks this planet . . . not just us single folks.

2. **Our lives don't serve a purpose unless we're in a relationship.** We matter. We *matter*. We have precious gifts to offer the world that have nothing whatsoever to do with our relationship status. We might be single, but we are not "singular" in any way. We are multidimensional, unique, talented, purposeful, meaningful people with hugely

important lives and destinies. A relationship can certainly bring us great happiness and fulfillment and even new purpose and meaning . . . but we are here to bring those very things to the world around us, just as we are. And sometimes our unattached, unencumbered single lives can have even *more* purpose than our future married lives, because we are able to wholeheartedly and without distraction pursue our passions, our calling, our dreams, our greater purpose. A relationship can someday add to that, but it cannot and will not ever define or replace your greater purpose. There is something you and only you are meant to do with your life that isn't dependent on a relationship to make it happen. Like I always say, you don't need a significant other to lead a significant life.

3. **We have to wait around for a relationship to realize our destiny.** It's time to stop waiting and start *living*. Yes, two people coming together is a beautiful thing . . . but so is one person standing boldly in their purpose. You don't have to sit idly by, waiting for the day that a prince comes riding up on his white horse and the two of you gallop off into the sunset of your destiny. Your destiny is in the here and now. God wants to do something powerful with you and for you and through you now. Today. This moment. I don't know what it is, I can't possibly tell you what your destiny on this planet is, but I *can* tell you that had I not made the choice to follow my passion and chase my dreams and pour my heart and soul into making the world around me a better place right where I was . . . you wouldn't be reading this book right now. I had to get past my singleness and decide that I had things to do with my life, and I didn't have time to wait around on a man to come along for me to do them. I hope with all my heart that someday someone *will* come along and join me in

my journey, but I'm not going to hit the Pause button on my life until that happens (although I do reserve the right to hit the Pause button on my dating life from time to time). And you shouldn't either. Do all the things you want to do with your life *right now*. Stop waiting. Because the truth is, a woman who creates a full, joyful, meaningful life for herself is a lot more appealing (and happy) than a woman who waits around on a man to do it for her.

RULE TO Re-meme-ber

When you get to the heart of the matter, we're *all* flawed in our own unique ways, married and single people alike . . . so, to take a single woman and have her turn inward on herself and question her very worth and value and character just because she happens to *be* a single woman is wrong and damaging and unfair. Maybe we should all just back up off the rhetoric a little and let single people be. Let married people be. Let us all be free in our own unique experience of life, love, and the pursuit of happiness, whatever that happens to look like for each of us. Maybe for some it's 2.5 kids and a picket fence. Maybe for me it's two cats and a downtown condo. And that doesn't make you better or me worse or you wrong and me right. It just makes us *different*.

Let's give each other the freedom to be different. And while we're at it, let's give OURSELVES permission to be different too. It's time. Things have changed. Families look different. Happiness looks different. The era has passed when Barbie needed Ken to buy her dream house or even to build her dream house. Shouldn't we step outta the way and give her the freedom to build her dream *life* and then decide if she wants to invite Ken to join her?

Let's give each other the freedom to be different. And while we're at it, let's give OURSELVES permission to be different too.

20

Livin' la Vida Solo

One Is the Loneliest Number . . . or Is It?

In the life of every single girl, she will, on occasion, find herself at a very important crossroads. She makes plans with a friend to go to dinner at the latest great restaurant in town and the friend backs out at the last minute. She wants to see the sappy chick flick that just hit theaters, since sappy chick flicks are somewhat of a rarity these days, and none of her BFFs have a free afternoon. Or she has a week off work when everyone else is up to their eyeballs in deadlines, and she has no one to join her on a carpe diem road trip. She has two choices when one of these incidents occurs: (A) cancel her plans, thereby missing the great restaurant, movie, or date with the open road, or (B) pack up her independence, go by herself, and *werk it.*

The obvious arguments against choosing option B are "I'll look desperate, like I have no friends," or "I'll feel stupid," or "I won't have anyone to talk to." The easy option, the path of least resistance, is option A. But if you want to embrace your singleness, get comfortable with your solidarity, learn to enjoy your own company, and stop letting the swipe rule your life . . . the clear choice is to stop hiding behind excuses and take yourself out on the town without fear or hesitation. At the end of the day, if you can't learn to enjoy your own company, how can you expect anyone else to?

One of the best vacations I ever experienced was one that my mom and I took a few years ago to Wilmington, North Carolina. My mom accidentally left most of her luggage at home and didn't feel comfortable flitting all over town in the one pair of gym shorts or the one bathing suit that made it on the trip. (How we managed to leave an entire suitcase behind is still a mystery.) So she opted to spend most of her time at the beach house, soaking up the sun with a good book, while I explored the town by myself. And you know what? It was one of the greatest, most fun, most empowering experiences of my life. Essentially on vacation alone, I was forced to step outside my comfort zone and talk to people I might not ordinarily talk to because I didn't have anyone there as a safety net. Plus, I got to be an extra on *Dawson's Creek*! (For the second time . . . you might have read about the first time in *I've Never Been to Vegas but My Luggage Has*.) Whether on set filming or out and about exploring the town, my walls came down, strangers became friends, and a new sense of independence was born—one that has stayed with me ever since. Because let's face it: if you can spend an hour or a day or a week in the company of yourself and have the time of your life, there ain't nothin' you can't do.

Here are a few rules to abide by when hitting the town as a party of one:

- DO go big or go home. Don't slink into the cheap diner on the corner or the bad movie that no one else is at because you don't want anyone to see you alone. You're defeating the purpose, which is to flaunt your independence and celebrate your bossbabe status—not to keep it under wraps. Go to the restaurant you want to go to (you know, the new hot spot in town that everybody's talking about). Go with boldness and confidence, not with worry of who might see you there alone. Make reservations . . . don't take reservations.

- DON'T hide behind a cell phone, a laptop, or a really big pair of sunglasses. Don't pretend to be mesmerized by your Twitter feed to avoid making eye contact with the cute guy at the table beside you for fear of what he'll think of you being alone. Look him in the eye and dare him to *not* find you fabulous. The truth is, a woman without defenses and roadblocks is often much more appealing to a man than a woman buried beneath a gaggle of girlfriends.
- DO look cute. Just because you're a party of one doesn't mean you shouldn't dress to impress. Don't make the effort to attract a man—make the effort for *you*. Why? Because you are worthy of the very best! Wear that little black dress you've been saving for a special occasion. What better excuse to break out that new pair of stilettos than to march to the beat of your own drummer? Besides, that guy flying solo two seats down from you will notice—and a party of one might quickly be upgraded to a party of two. (But if it's not, that's perfectly okay too.)
- DON'T sit at the table, at the bar, or in the theater with a panic-stricken, deer-in-headlights look on your face. Relax. Breathe. Smile. Engage with your surroundings. This is fun! You are your own best friend . . . and who doesn't love an evening out on the town with their best friend?
- DO talk to strangers. A stranger is only a "hello" away from becoming a friend. The best way to meet new people and have new adventures is by stepping outside

> your comfort zone and opening yourself up to the unknown. There are fascinating stories all around you just waiting to be told—so stop playing it so safe and go walk on the edge for a little while. The view's much better from up there.

At the end of the day, you're not always going to have a plus one to accompany you through life—and that's okay. But don't believe the swipe! One is only the loneliest number if you don't like the company. A single and fabulous lady like yourself doesn't need a partner in crime to enjoy everything that flying solo through life has to offer. One of my very favorite self-care activities has become taking myself on a date to the movies. I love it. I get a jumbo box of Junior Mints, bring a big fuzzy blanket, and reserve a seat in the top corner all by myself. Then I kick off my shoes, kick back in my recliner, and let the action on the big screen transport me to my happy place. It's completely relaxing and therapeutic and energizing, and I always leave the theater happier than when I came. It's gotten to the point where I almost enjoy going to movies alone more than I do with someone else! And it's a healing, empowering thing—learning to love your own company. I encourage you to find your own solo self-care routine, whether it's going to the movies, the gym, or the bookstore or going shopping or whatever . . . and make it a regular date! Pretty soon, you'll be looking forward to it just like you would any other social engagement.

Remember, not every table you choose to sit at in life is going to be a poker game already in progress, with people on both sides of you. Sometimes you're going to find that a single deck of cards and a game of solitaire is the hand you've been dealt. Are you going to let that stop you from winning the game?

RULE TO Re-meme-ber

Your challenge for this weekend: Do one thing alone. Go sit in a coffee shop and read a great book. Go check out that new art exhibit at the museum. Go for a hike. Spend some time with *you*, take *you* out on a date, learn to love hanging out with *you*! Stop waiting on other people to do the things you want to do and love to do, and get out there and do them! You don't need anyone to bring you happiness . . . you can go out there and get it yourself. You might be surprised at how much you enjoy your own company. Remember: you don't need a cosigner, because you're not a house; you don't need anyone to validate you, because you're not a car; and you don't need anyone to complete you, because you are *not* Jerry Maguire! Now get out there and treat yo' solo self!

Stop waiting on other people to do the things you want to do and love to do, and get out there and do them! You don't need anyone to bring you happiness . . . you can go out there and get it yourself.

21

Party of You

Why We Should Throw Showers for Singles Too

I've spent the greater part of the past decade examining what it means to be single. And pointing out all the many positive aspects of single life. And leading the "Single & Fabulous" parade down the Main Street of Twitter, Facebook, Instagram, Pinterest, the internet, and any other social media outlet that would listen. And generally being the poster child for shiny, happy singleness. And you know what? That's awesome, and I'm proud of the work I've done to help flip the script on single life so that women (and men) learn to accept their relationship status as just another part of who they are rather than viewing it as this great big, scary thing.

But you know what else? I'm growing weary of spending countless hours writing about all the reasons why we singletons should "accept" our singleness . . . and posting daily reminders about why singleness isn't "that bad" . . . and feeling like I'm having to constantly put a positive spin on a negative situation. Why is our singleness viewed as a negative thing to begin with? Who gets to determine that for us? Society? Pop culture? Married people? Did *we* label it as negative? Why are we made to feel less than or lacking or incomplete just because we happen to check the box marked "Single" on tax forms and job applications?

And then it occurred to me the other day . . . almost like a light bulb going off above my head as I sat and pondered my singleness, and the answer became crystal clear.

Why does singleness have this overwhelmingly negative connotation? Because we don't celebrate our singles. Like, at all.

We just don't. I mean, yeah . . . we have birthdays, of course . . . but who over the age of about twenty-five really makes a big deal out of their birthday? And besides, everybody has a birthday, so that doesn't count.

We simply don't celebrate our singles. We celebrate our couples for making the decision to get married. We celebrate them again once they actually *get* married. We celebrate their choice to start a family (and then celebrate them again and again and sometimes again and again and again when they decide to expand that family). We celebrate the anniversaries of their marriages and the christenings and baptisms of their babies and their kids' birthdays and their buying of a new home or choosing to adopt. Sometimes we even celebrate when they decide to end their marriage. But we simply don't celebrate our singles.

We singles buy gifts we can't afford and take off work to get fitted for endless numbers of (mostly unflattering) bridesmaids' dresses and budget for housewarming presents, birthday presents, anniversary presents, graduation presents, shower presents, and on and on and on . . . all in the name of being supportive of our married friends' life choices. And that's a beautiful thing. But why aren't *our* choices being celebrated?

Where was the party when I ended my ten-year, on-again/off-again, mostly toxic relationship? Or when I achieved my lifelong goal of hitting the *New York Times* bestseller list? Where was the celebratory shower when my friend Anetra won an Emmy or my friend William got a major promotion or my friend Cindy quit her steady, dependable, salaried job, along with its benefits and 401(k), to pursue her dreams in the music industry?

Where was the parade down Main Street when you bought your first condo or lost twenty pounds or went back to school or adopted a child as a single woman or walked away from that dead-end job or told that loser ex to take a hike or overcame depression? Where was the big party or shower or celebration to commemorate those beautiful, brave, bold life choices?

There's a quote that says, "You're not single because something is wrong with you. You are single because you are single. It's really as simple as that." I'm not sure who said that, but I say "Yassssss, queen (or king)!" There's not some deep, dark, mysterious, terrible reason why you're still single, and singleness is not a curse, a disease, or a punishment. It's time we stop acting like it is. If marriage is honored as a life choice, why isn't singleness? Singleness wasn't thrust upon us. It's not some horrible disease we woke up with one day. We're not just idling around, stewing in our own lonely misery, and waiting for the day when someone comes along and marries us and gives our lives meaning. Every day we are doing great big, scary, amazing things, and we are doing them *all alone*! And that is something to be recognized and commended and celebrated.

According to the life plan I came up with for myself when I was all of twenty-two (and utterly clueless about life), I'm "supposed" to be married with kids and a minivan and a house with a white picket fence right now. But instead I'm single with no kids and a car instead of a minivan and an apartment with no white picket fence in sight. But guess what? I love my life and I love my non-minivan and I love my cozy little apartment and I love this moment that I'm in right now. The way I see it, you can waste every precious minute of your life wishing to be somewhere else, doing something else . . . or you can simply toss out your own "life plan" and celebrate *this* season to the fullest—this beautifully uncertain, wild, magical, imperfect season of becoming a party of you before you become a party of two.

We have to stop spending our life waiting to be set free from this "prison" called singleness so we can finally join the ranks of celebrated coupledom. If society won't throw the party for us, let's throw it ourselves! Our unfinished, unwritten, imperfect lives deserve to be honored. Our life choices deserve to be recognized. And our singleness should be celebrated. We're doing this life thing just fine alone, and if that isn't brave and admirable and confetti-worthy, then I don't know what is.

I urge you to find a way to celebrate yourself and your singleness on a regular basis. Decide that you are going to be happy no matter what. Decide that you are going to make your dreams come true no matter what. And if those dreams include things like adopting a child and buying a house and doing things that people usually wait to do 'til they're married . . . I want you to do them anyway. I want you to stop *waiting* and start *living*. Stop waiting for love, stop waiting for marriage, stop waiting for Prince Charming to come along and rescue you, and start designing a life you don't wish to be rescued from. Life is short, and it's high time to decide that, alone or accompanied, you are going to build the most beautiful life you can, and then you are going to revel in it. Because, guess what? *You* are the one you've been waiting for. *You* are the one who can make your dreams come true. *You* are the one, the only one, you will 100 percent definitely spend the rest of your life with . . . and it's time to start making *you* happy. Not as a New Year's resolution or at some lofty date in the future but right now. Because you are worthy of a beautiful life, and that beautiful life starts and ends with *you*. Don't just accept your singleness—honor it! Appreciate it. Revel in it. Throw a shower for yourself and register at Target and Starbucks if you want to. But don't keep wishing it away because you're hoping and praying and longing for marriage. Stop letting the swipe rule your life. And don't for one second allow society to cause you to believe that you don't lead a life that's worthy of celebrating. Whether your singleness is for a season or for a lifetime, there is great beauty, adventure, magic, love, laughter, and happiness right here in the middle of *this moment*. And I don't know about you, but I'd say that's worth a celebration or two.

RULE TO Re-meme-ber

Waiting for love.

Waiting for marriage.

Waiting to buy a house.

Waiting to travel.

Waiting to move to a new city.

Waiting to start a family.

Waiting to do, to be, to act, to *live*.

I say, no more.

Stop waiting for love and start *living*!

You have a great big beautiful life to live, and finding love is just one chapter. I am no longer waiting for anyone to do anything! In the next year or so, I am planning to buy a house, to start exploring adoption as a single woman, to move into the next chapter of my life, whether anyone joins me in it or not. I'm going to stop waiting for other people to celebrate me and my life, and I'm going to start celebrating myself. Life is precious and should be lived to the very last drop, whether you are walking alone or with a partner. Make today the day you stop planning all the things you're going to do once you've found a mate and start doing them! And then throw a party in your own honor. I'll bring the Chex Mix.

Life is precious and should be lived to the very last drop, whether you are walking alone or with a partner.

22

Serial Seek*hers*

Guys Who Find You but Keep Looking

When I emerged from my dating hiatus after six months, I felt like Punxsutawney Phil emerging from deep hibernation. When it had started, it was early spring. When it ended, it was mid-fall. It was a new season for me, literally and figuratively. My gut told me that it was time to get back out there. I wanted to try a new dating app, so I got my profile up and I was off to the races. Although it had only been six months, things change so fast in modern dating, it might as well have been six years. I was brand new at the game once again, and it was exciting and scary and exhilarating and terrifying all at once. I felt like I was newborn cub Simba and the dating app was Mufasa, thrusting me out onto the dating scene to be introduced to and inspected by the world. And as I blinked and stretched and slowly found my dating legs again, I was dismayed to discover an entirely new type of man had emerged in my absence: the seekher. No, not the "seeker." The seek*her*.

It all started with a date with a guy who seemed to have a lot of potential. He and I had very similar professional backgrounds. He was cute. He was funny. He was great at the witty banter (wit is my love language). He was the right age. He seemed established and grounded in his career and in who he was. I was excited to meet him for dinner. I was less excited when he suggested meeting for an extra early dinner. That reeked of "double-booker" to me. (Or heck, maybe even the rare *triple*-booker!) If you refer back to our Modern Dating Dictionary, you'll recall that a double-booker is someone who books more than one date in one day. I have been guilty of being a double-booker once or twice in my own dating history, but it's not something I do regularly because, frankly, it's exhausting—especially if it's two first dates back-to-back—going through the whole litany of "getting to know you" questions. Since I myself had been a double-booker in the past, I knew I couldn't be too offended if that's what Ron Burgundy (since his background was in news, that's what we'll call him) was doing. However, he was so incredibly persistent about the fact that he wanted to meet super early because he vaguely "had other plans later," it was a bit off-putting. It didn't feel like dinner at all! It was "slunch," as my mom jokingly refers to the meal between lunch and supper. I wanted to give him the benefit of the doubt since this was my first date spawned from this new dating app, and I wanted to keep a positive attitude. (At least until the app sucked every bit of my will to live right out of me, as dating apps have been known to do, LOL!)

Anyway, the day of our date arrived, and Ron Burgundy and I met up at a little restaurant halfway between his place and mine. Things seemed to get off to a great start. The conversation flowed easily, laughter abounded, and we definitely had a lot in common. I started to see the first inklings of a potential connection.

But as dinner progressed, I began to feel like I was on a date with that kid on the baseball team who's staring around the outfield at butterflies instead of at the ball—me being the ball and

Ron Burgundy's phone, our surroundings, his watch, and basically everything other than me being the butterflies. He got increasingly twitchy and restless as the date went on. He glanced at his watch every thirty seconds or so. He stopped midconvo a couple of times to respond to texts. It was difficult to maintain a train of thought as I answered his questions because he would ask them and then start chasing butterflies again. And these were *not* the kind of butterflies you hope for on a first date.

Ron had barely touched his food when he interrupted me literally in midsentence to interject: "I hate to cut you off, but I really have to be going or I won't make my next event." It was glaringly apparent that he had a second date, probably dinner number two of the evening. And the thing is, I don't think it would have mattered if we had shown up to that date and both fallen madly in love on the spot. I think Ron would have still chased butterflies the whole time and torn out of that restaurant faster than the roadrunner in pursuit of the coyote to make it to date number two (which I'm guessing ended promptly at 8:00, when date number three began).

Was Ron Burgundy's abrasive and sketchy behavior due to the fact that he simply wasn't that into me? It's possible. But I believe the real reason is that Ronnie B. is a seekher. To save you the trouble of flipping back to our Modern Dating Dictionary, a seekher is a newly evolved variety of man who monkeys his way through connection after connection, date after date, relationship after relationship at lightning pace, ever seeking but never finding. He's only comfortable *looking* for love and not actually finding it because if he found it, he would have to commit to someone. This man *says* he wants to find his dream woman, but the truth is, he'd much prefer the safety of continuing to seek her for the rest of his life over the danger of actually finding her. Evolving during the dating app generation, a seekher is so seduced by the swipe, he'd rather spend his life scrolling through seemingly endless options than picking and committing to just one.

That's why a seekher can be out with an amazing woman and still focus more on his phone alerting him to potential prospects than on the real prospect sitting right in front of him. To him, the grass is always greener. Seekhers are always searching for something: a different job, a different friend group, a different city, a different person to date. The search is their comfort zone. The finding . . . well, the finding is something else altogether. The finding scares them. The finding means they might have to give themselves—all of themselves, the good and the bad—over to someone else and risk that person hurting or leaving them. The finding means they have to let someone see them, and that terrifies them. The finding means they can no longer dodge or run or evade or hide but that they have to just stand still and let someone get to know them. They're not ready to do that. So they keep scrolling. They keep hiding out in the swipe. And they're so clever about it, they can almost make themselves and everyone else believe that they're just restless, they're just looking for a place to fit, and they don't really know exactly what it is they're looking for, but they know they haven't yet found it.

Some seekhers will attempt to keep you in their life with the safe label of "friend." That allows them to still have you in their life, which they want, without having to go all in with you, which they're not ready to do. In hindsight, I realized Chandler Bing was a seekher. Seekhers are terrified to go all in with one person, so they go partially in with five or six people. They double- and triple-book dates and only halfway show up to each one because their mind is already on the next date. Seekhers prefer to stay in the shallow end of the dating pool because the shallow doesn't require them to risk or feel or love. They need the shallow and the safe and the search because letting go of the search would require a level of commitment they're not ready for. Seekhers are always on the lookout for the next best thing. And because they're never satisfied, they will never find the next best thing, which is a good thing, because they don't really want to find it. They are way too energized by the endless thrill of the chase.

Trying to date a seekher is like trying to date that dude from the infamous meme who's walking with one girl (seemingly his girlfriend) and stops in his tracks to turn around and ogle another one. And who wants their love life to be a live-action meme? Seekhers are the most exhausting form of modern dater and will leave you feeling frustrated and confused and like you simply aren't enough when, really, *they're* not enough for you. How could they be? They're spreading themselves too thin with five or six women to ever be enough for just one.

I don't know about you, but I'm tired of being searched for.

I am ready to be found.

When Ron Burgundy and I parted ways that day (quickly, because he had ants in his pants), we hugged and exchanged pleasantries, and he said, "We should do this again sometime." But, of course, we didn't. He texted me halfheartedly a few times after our date, but our communication fizzled out, as I'm sure he got distracted by the latest five women he had swiped right on. And you know what? That's okay. I was no longer letting the swipe rule my life. Once upon a time, I had used dating and the way men were treating me as a metric for how I viewed myself and my worth. After my dating break, I knew that my worth was a fixed point and had nothing whatsoever to do with anyone other than *me*. And because my worth had increased, and because I was dating from a whole place and not an empty place . . . I didn't need to be found by Ron Burgundy or by any other seekher. I had found myself. I was no longer shaken by the ups and downs of dating, because I loved myself and I knew what I brought to the table and I knew that I was worthy of more than someone who sat down at that table with me and chased butterflies instead of my heart. My dating hiatus was exactly what I needed in order to get back to myself and learn how to be content with me and my path before looking for someone to join me on it.

If you are dating as a glass half empty and searching for someone to fill you up today . . . I want to remind you that your worth has nothing to do with who's *beside* you and everything to do with what's *inside* you. You are not defined by the swipe. You don't need a man to find you. You don't need a man to complete you. You only need to find yourself and complete yourself . . . and then you'll be ready for a relationship to be the cherry on top.

RULE TO Re-meme-ber

This one's for the gentlemen or, more specifically, the seekhers of the world. Here's the thing: if you're always on the lookout for "the bigger, better deal," you can rest assured that while you might find it (prettier, smarter, skinnier, younger, etc.), you will never be truly satisfied with it. This is not saying you should settle by any means, but if you'd rather spend your life searching than finding . . . you're signing up for a life of loneliness and misery. Put your phone away and invest in the woman right in front of you, guys. Because only a boy treats every woman he meets like an option. A man makes one great woman his choice and doesn't let FOMO (fear of missing out) cause him to miss out on an amazing thing.

Only a boy treats every woman he meets like an option. A man makes one great woman his choice and doesn't let FOMO (fear of missing out) cause him to miss out on an amazing thing.

23

Know Your Value (Meal)

Fries Are a Side Item, You Are Not

Another species that has emerged from the era of modern dating, which you've no doubt heard of because it's been around a lot longer than the seekher, is the side chick. The side chick is also commonly known as *the side piece* or *the side item* or *the side dish*. Back in the day, we used the term *the other woman*, but nowadays the internet seems to assign a newfangled word to everything. A side chick/side piece/side item/side dish is someone a man keeps around as a plan B—a backup plan or a second fiddle—to the main chick. Most of the time side chicks are unwittingly side chicks, but some women are sadly and knowingly content to play second fiddle to another woman as long as it means they get to be in the band.

Let's use this analogy. You sit down for dinner at your favorite boujee restaurant. You take your time poring over that menu to find the most delicious, most expensive, most savory item the restaurant has to offer because, hey, if you're going to invest that kind of money, you should make sure you order only the best (or at least what you view as the best), right? So, chances are you're not too concerned about the steamed broccoli that comes with it. Sure, the broccoli might look pretty and add some color to the plate, and it might get your attention, at least for a few minutes, after you've finished your steak or possibly even between bites. But if the server comes along and scoops up your plate with a few pieces of broccoli left on it, you're probably not going to miss it all that much. Why? Because you were so utterly satisfied by that oh-so-tasty steak that the broccoli was merely an afterthought. Translation: in a relationship, you want to always be the steak, because if you're not, chances are you're the broccoli or—to be blunt—the side dish that your man can live without.

Now, you might be asking yourself, *Just who is* she *to tell me that I am not my man's main course?*

I might not be Dr. Phil, but I can tell you that, unlike Dr. Phil, I have been the side chick a few times in my life. I've been the side chick without even realizing I was the side chick. In fact, not only did I think I was the main chick, I thought I was the *only* chick. And I have tons of single girlfriends who have also been cast in the side piece role and ignored the many, many signs that there was someone else sitting pretty in the main chick role. The guys who are doing all this chick . . . multitasking . . . are not necessarily bad guys (although sometimes they are), but you know what I call a guy who juggles multiple women? A clown. And I can promise you that once that clown has filed you away in the side item drawer, you will never, ever be more than the French fries to the main dish's cheeseburger.

If you're pretty sure he likes it but he still hasn't put a ring on it, this one is for you. To save you many frustrating years of waiting for your boo to pull that small black velvet box out of his coat pocket, only to find a pair of earrings or—God forbid—a keychain, I have put together a handy little list of ways to tell if you are not the main dish but are instead . . . *dum da dum dum* . . . the side item.

Take a deep breath, muster up your courage, and pull around to the second window, because if your guy fits one or more of these descriptions, you might have found yourself in a French fry situation:

1. He only hits you up at 2:00 a.m. instead of 2:00 p.m. Yep, if he only comes knockin' after the clubs have stopped rockin' . . . check the menu, girl, 'cause you'll probably find your name right next to the broccoli. Possible exceptions to this rule: you're dating someone who works nights . . . or you're dating a vampire. And since I hear Robert Pattinson has hung up his sparkly vampire suit for a Batman cape, this exception probably doesn't apply.
2. When it comes to texting, he's shadier than a pool umbrella. This is a true story and it involves Chandler Bing—again, the fake Chandler Bing and not the real one (well, technically, I guess they're both fake . . . but you know what I mean): When Chandler Bing would text me while he was with his main chick (I had no clue that she even existed), he would send me a text and immediately put his phone on airplane mode. Since we had the same type of phone, I would get confused that, pretty frequently, my responses to him would go through as green text messages instead of iMessages, especially when I would text him back almost immediately.

   Finally I asked him, "Do you text me sometimes and then immediately throw your phone into a ravine?" and I explained to him my reason for asking. He got all flustered and stammered and sputtered out some nonsensical response, and I was left even more flummoxed by this weird texting glitch.

   Until one day as I was explaining the situation to one of my girlfriends and she stopped me midsentence. "Mandy, you realize what he's doing, right?" Clearly, I didn't realize what he was doing or I wouldn't be puzzling over it. She went on: "When you turn your phone on airplane mode, it keeps texts from coming through until you turn it *off* airplane mode. I'm guessing when he's with another girl, he waits 'til she's distracted or in the bathroom or whatever, then he sends you a text. But he doesn't want your response to come through when he's sitting there next to her, so he puts his phone on airplane mode until she walks away again and he can let your response come through without her ever being the wiser."

I was floored. What kind of sorcery was this? Would any human being go to such ridiculous lengths to juggle two women?! The obvious question was, Why did he text me at all when he was with another woman? Why not just wait until he's alone? My friend looked at me witheringly. "Mandy. Because *he's a man*."

I probably would have thought her theory was completely off the wall had I not brought it up with Chandler Bing the next time I saw him in person and watched him turn into the cat that swallowed the canary right in front of my very eyes. For someone so wily at covering his digital tracks, when confronted in person, he would crumble like a house of cards. He was doing the absolute most to try to ensure that his side chick and his main chick never crossed paths. I'm not even sure who was the side chick and who was the main chick in the equation. I'm not sure Chandler Bing was either. But what I am sure of is this: when a guy exhibits shady texting habits . . . there's a strong chance you're in a "Would you like fries with that?" situation. Possible exception: he really does text you and immediately throw his phone into a ravine.

3. You have him on an "every other weekend and holidays" status. I mean, c'mon, he's not a child, a dog, or

a houseplant. If your relationship feels like a constant custody battle, ask yourself who you are fighting with. Could it be he's spending the rest of his time with a main dish and you've been side-itemed? Possible exceptions: he travels a lot for work, he has kids from a previous relationship whom he spends his time with when he's not with you, or he regularly experiences alien abductions.

4. You've never met a friend, family member, or coworker of his . . . even though he's met all of yours. In other words, he's a total pocketer. If he's keeping you away from the people in his life or taking you three counties over to see a movie that's playing at five different theaters in town, you can bet you are the cheese and not the nachos . . . the butter and not the popcorn . . . the Junior and not the Mints. If he knows all your girlfriends' full names, dates of birth, and favorite Netflix shows, and you don't even know his address, Waze your way outta there, lady, 'cause there's somebody else he's going home to every night. Possible exceptions: he either has no friends or he's in the Witness Protection Program. In either case, you should probably still head for the hills.
5. He displays social media shadiness. You know what I'm talking about—he hides all his comments, deletes your tagged photos, won't change his relationship status, or in some cases, won't even accept your friend request. Or, he blocks you. Yes, a guy once blocked me on FB and had me convinced it was because it was too hard for *him* to see *my* page. (You know, the more examples I offer up from that situationship, the more I judge myself for not walking away sooner than I did. If you wanna see your life and especially your love life clearly—write a book!) Ladies, if he's hiding you, it's for a reason. Get out before

it's too late and he changes his status to "In a relationship with [a name that's not yours]." There are no exceptions to this rule.

If you've reached the end of this list and you know in your heart that your guy has you on carryout status and is going home to his dine-in, don't despair. Here's the good news: you figured it out! You caught on to his game before it was too late and you found yourself waking up in five years with nothing to show for the relationship but a bunch of McDonald's receipts and a broken heart. Remember, fries are a side item, but *you* are not! Just because he treated you like a side dish doesn't mean you are one. There's someone out there who will appreciate you and treat you as not only his main dish but his appetizer, salad, dessert, and after-dinner mint.

RULE TO Re-meme-ber

It feels like there are *way* too many women who are content to accept any scrap or crumb a man throws her way, so long as he keeps throwing *something* her way. Women are signing up to be someone's side item just so they get to have a place at the table, no matter how small. Ladies, it might be time to get up and leave that table if love and effort and respect and attentiveness are no longer being served. Stop settling for fast-food love when you deserve five-star love. A man who side-chicks you, who juggles you with multiple other women, and who offers you nothing but dishonesty, shadiness, and unfaithfulness is not a man who truly wants to be with you. Honor *you* by saying "Check, please!" And make sure you take your dignity with you when you go.

It might be time to get up and leave that table if love and effort and respect and attentiveness are no longer being served.

24

How Will I Know If He Really Loves Me?

Here's How to Know He Doesn't

Let me pause for a second and geekily revel in the fact that I managed to work one of my favorite Whitney Houston songs of all time into the title of this chapter.

Okay . . . back to the business at hand, because it's important business.

One of the most frequent questions I get from my readers is "How do I know if he really loves me and wants to be with me?" It makes me sad that so many wonderfully deserving and quality women out there are in situationships or relationships where they even have to ask this question. And still, I hear it all the time. From readers, from friends, across social media, and Lord knows, I've heard the same cry from my own heart at least a dozen times: *"How do I know if he really loves me and wants to be with me?"*

Sadly, I can't give you some magic formula to figure out if he loves you and wants to be with you. I can't tell you this because

I have yet to find my forever person who I hope will answer this question for me. But through my own experiences and through helping many a friend navigate their way through many a heartache . . . I think I have come up with a pretty clear formula to tell if he *doesn't* really love you or want to be with you. Which might sound harsh until I remind you that a man who doesn't love you and doesn't want to be with you is also a man who doesn't deserve you.

So here goes.

A man who doesn't love you and doesn't want to be with you will constantly leave you questioning everything about the relationship. There will be no certainty, no solid ground. Everything will be fraught with hesitation and doubt and anxiety. He will purposely leave you idling in the gray area as long as you are content to stay there so he feels safe in the knowledge that he always has a standby if and when the need arises. You will constantly be walking on quicksand or eggshells. You will constantly struggle to find your footing. He will give a little, then take away a lot. You will never feel safe in the relationship. The moment you start to feel safe, he'll jerk the rug out from under you to remind you that he is in control, not you.

A man who doesn't love you and doesn't want to be with you will drift in and out of your life on his own accord and his own timetable. He'll leave you feeling as though his doing this is a huge favor to you. He will breadcrumb you and come around just often enough to keep you hanging on without really offering you anything of substance, like time and effort. He will subtly let you know, when he does actually invest in the relationship, that time spent with you is not a privilege but an inconvenience to him . . . so you should savor every precious moment he allots to you because you weren't worthy of it in the first place. (He'll do this so subtly, in fact, that it will almost seem charming.) Here's the thing, though: a man who doesn't love you and doesn't want to be with you will never, ever *really* inconvenience himself for you. He will never meet you halfway. You will be left to do all the work, all the heavy lifting, all the effort. And you keep doing it because you know if you don't, you'll never get to see him.

A man who doesn't love you and doesn't want to be with you will never ask you how your day was. Nope . . . small gestures of thoughtfulness like that aren't even on his radar. The truth is, he doesn't ask you how your day was because he doesn't care to hear the answer.

A man who doesn't love you and doesn't want to be with you will dodge. He will never give a straight answer. He will act shady. He will disappear for long intervals of time. He will zombie you over and over and over again. He's always "crazy busy." He won't respond to texts in a timely fashion or at all. He will leave you on read for days at a time. His phone constantly "dies" or he is perpetually "out of service" (or secretly on airplane mode). He will be largely unavailable to you . . . always emotionally and often literally. He will lie to you. He will cancel plans at the last minute. He will leave you waiting for hours. You are more likely to hear from him at 2:00 a.m. than 2:00 p.m. He won't introduce you to his friends. You won't see any sign of yourself on his social media pages. He will act single regardless of what his Facebook status says.

And after a certain amount of all of the above and of slowly having your dignity, confidence, and self-esteem chipped away a little at a time . . . a man who doesn't love you and doesn't want to be with you will leave you questioning everything about yourself. He will have you completely allowing the swipe to rule your life. Why aren't you enough for him? Why are his friends more important than you? Why is his work more important than you? Why did you dare speak up and tell him that he hurt your feelings? That's probably why you haven't heard from him in weeks. What is he doing behind your back? What is he doing when he vanishes from your life? Why are you not worthy of his time, love, and attention? What can you do better to make him love you more? Why does he act ashamed to post anything about you on his social media pages? Are you too fat? Too old? Too ugly? Too insecure? Too needy? Too independent? Too *much*?

(The answer to all those questions is a resounding no, with the exception of the last question. Yes, you are too much. Too much woman for that too little man.)

But finally . . . all this evidence means nothing, because you already answered your question when you asked it.

"How do I know if he loves me and wants to be with me?"

You know because you will never have to ask that question of a man who does.

RULE TO Re-meme-ber

Please understand that when someone acts like they don't care, they genuinely don't care. This is a painful realization, but it can also be a freeing one. Give yourself permission to stop. Stop texting, stop asking, definitely stop begging, and . . . let it go. Let it be. Let *him* be. You deserve better than someone who doesn't return your love. You deserve better than someone who's breadcrumbing or zombie-ing or ghosting or cheating on you. You deserve better than someone you have to ask to love you.

So often I get emails from ladies asking me why they weren't "enough" to keep a man interested or keep him from cheating or keep him from ghosting . . . and it pains me that we always seem to internalize the bad behavior of others and blame ourselves rather than recognizing that it wasn't about us. It was never about us. Other people's shortcomings are not your fault. What if it wasn't that you weren't "enough"? What if it was that you were *too* much? Too amazing? Too successful? Too confident? Too bold? Too smart? Too witty? Too incredible? So much so that the other person bailed because of their own inadequacies and not yours? Sometimes you just have to let people go; recognize that they are not capable of rising up to your level and let them go. But don't believe the swipe and let their insecurities become yours. You are exactly as you should be. Not perfect . . . but wonderfully, beautifully, perfectly enough.

Here is what it all boils down to: If a man loves you and wants to be with you, he will be with you. You won't have to jump through hoops. You won't have to complete obstacle courses. You won't have to online stalk him (or any of his exes). You won't have to slide into the DMs of the girl he used to date or is currently dating to mark your territory. You won't have to send him text messages longer than a CVS receipt, detailing all the reasons he's a fool not to see what he has standing right in front of him. You won't have to post thirst-trap selfies or passive-aggressive quotes on social media to get his attention. You won't have to show up every weekend at his gym/Starbucks/grocery store/etc. to "accidentally" run into him even though it's on the other side of town from you. You won't have to manipulate, plot, scheme, or force interactions of any kind. You won't have to stay on his radar at all.

Also, if a man loves you and wants to be with you, he won't break up with you. He won't cheat on you. He won't hide you or lie to you or ghost you. Since he's not on a cell phone plan from the early 2000s, you won't hear from him only at night and on weekends. He won't be shadier than a pool umbrella. His social media pages won't be wiped clean of you. And his status won't say "Single" while yours says "In a relationship." If a man wants to be with you . . . HE WILL BE WITH YOU. Online and in real time. It's not rocket science. This is not a gray area. It's black and white, cut and dried.

So please, please take this tough love rant of mine as your sign to stop tap dancing to get his attention. Stop bending over backwards to make him see you. Stop texting him while he leaves you on read. Stop reminding him that you exist. If you have to fight to stay in his line of sight . . . #thankunext. He is not the man for you.

If a man wants to be with you . . .
HE WILL BE WITH YOU. Online and in real time. It's not rocket science. This is not a gray area. It's black and white, cut and dried.

25

Breaking Up Is Hard to Do

How to Lose Love without Losing Yourself

Back in the day (which was only, like, ten years ago), when a relationship ended, you could part ways with someone and be relatively certain you could avoid seeing them. Stay away from their favorite hangouts, avoid the grocery store where they shop, find a new gym. And while the once-every-blue-moon run-in might happen, for the most part, you knew geography was destiny and you could steer clear of your ex's neighborhood until the end of time if you needed to.

In today's technology-driven world, however, within the first two seconds of checking your phone in the morning, you might be besieged with one ex's engagement photos on Instagram, another updating his relationship status on Facebook, and yet another sharing his 280-character declaration of love for his new girlfriend on Twitter. Yes, it seems you can't leave the virtual house these days without bumping into one of your exes on the corner of Snapchat and TikTok. This can be particularly painful if your ex ghosted or Houdinied you but has now turned into the World's Best Boyfriend.

Breaking up is such a strange phenomenon in that someone who was part of your everyday life, someone who knows you better than perhaps anyone, someone you talked to and spent time with every single day . . . suddenly becomes someone you simply used to know.

If you're like me, when a relationship ends, you would be happy to ship your ex off to a deserted island, never to be seen or heard from again. Maybe to the same island that houses all our lost socks from the dryer. Or, in the words of Miranda Hobbes (*Sex and the City*), "I'd love to be all: 'We loved, thank you. You enriched my life, now go prosper.' But I'm more: 'We didn't work out. You need to not exist.'"

Unfortunately, since the Island of Misfit Boys doesn't exist, we're forced to learn to confront and coexist with our ghosts of relationships past, if not in real time, then at least online. So how do we do that? Here are my top ten tips for losing love without losing yourself:

1. First and foremost, realize that if the relationship ended, for whatever reason . . . it was not the relationship for you. Anyone who can walk away from you or let you walk away from them is not someone who was invested in your life to begin with.
2. Reflect on the red flags you might have ignored along the way. When I was dating Johnny Castle, the dude was wrapped in red flags. But I kept justifying my decision to date him with, "I'm looking at his heart and not his issues. We all have issues." This is a romantic concept in theory, but in reality, you've gotta look at his heart *and* his issues. And if he has more issues than *Vogue*, it's time to unsubscribe before you get any deeper into the relationship.

3. Have the final talk/exchanging of the personal belongings if you can . . . but don't let a lack of finality keep you stuck. You don't always get that final conversation, and you can't let a lack of closure keep you from moving on. If you have the kind of vibe with your ex that allows you to come together and talk things out and walk away peacefully, by all means—do it. It's always best to end things on a positive note. But sometimes that might not be possible, and it's up to you to find your own closure. You can't rely on someone else to give you every answer you need in order to move on. Sometimes there are no answers, simply questions . . . and you have to find a way to either live with or let go of those questions and not let them keep you trapped in relationship purgatory.
4. Don't be afraid to take a little social media detox following a heartbreak. Chances are, you could use the time and peace and quiet to heal anyway. You don't have to rush to make some grand announcement about the end of your relationship. (Don't you hate those extra cringey public Facebook declarations that they are no longer "In a relationship"?) Unless you're an actress, a princess, or one of the *Real Housewives*, there's no need to make a formal announcement about your split. And on that note, you might consider not announcing your relationship on social media until you're 100 percent sure it's the real deal. I say that because I made the mistake of going public with my last really serious relationship, only to turn around and have to recall everything I had posted a few months later. I'm not shaming myself or anyone who chooses to put their relationship online . . . I'm just saying sometimes a little discretion goes a long way. Everyone doesn't need to know every single detail of your life the moment something happens. Some things are

better kept close to your heart, at least until you know for sure that you're both in it for the long haul.

5. If you do stay online, don't post emo quote after emo quote or passive-aggressive meme after passive-aggressive meme. Believe me, I get the temptation to be petty, especially if your ex did you wrong. I can be Petty Crocker, Petty Boop, and Petty White all rolled into one sometimes. But at the end of the day, making constant online digs comes off as childish and a little desperate. When a relationship ends, you are better served by putting your dignity on display and taking the high road instead of trying to engage your ex in a war of memes. They don't get to be with you anymore and that is punishment enough.
6. Unfriend, unfollow, delete. You don't have to and shouldn't stay connected to your ex on social media immediately following a breakup, no matter how amicable the breakup was. Maybe at some distant time in the future you can reconnect as friends, but for now, when the wounds are still fresh—out of sight, out of mind is the best approach. But . . .
7. Don't block your ex . . . unless you have to. I'm of the opinion that blocking is in the same family with passive-aggressive memes. It just looks extra and overly dramatic. Disconnecting from them will accomplish the same thing without all the theatrics. One of my exes blocked me after we ended things, and I didn't find out until months later because I never went to his social media pages. When I did find out, it seemed over the top and silly. I was baffled. We had never been online friends on any platform, so what was the point? Also, to prove my above point about how I can sometimes be the unabashed Queen of Petty, why block them when you can instead force them

to watch you move on with your fabulous life? I mean, if they choose to stalk your pages, it's not your fault what they see. And what they should see is you living your best life, not blocking them out of some desperate need for attention or to get a reaction.

8. Make a clean break. Don't continue to hang out at the places where you know he'll be, don't try to stay friends with his friends, and don't find excuses to reach out to him every five minutes. You need time to heal and move forward with your new life, and you can't do that if you're still around him or talking to him or even just "accidentally" running into him every single day. Perhaps at some point in the future, you might be able to be friends with him, but for now, focus on you and healing your heart and becoming friends with yourself again. Chances are, if you've been in a serious relationship for any amount of time, you've probably neglected yourself and your self-care a bit anyway.
9. DO NOT STALK HIM ONLINE. This is where blocking might have to be put into play, if your browser seems to magically drift to his Instagram page every time you pick up your phone. If you need to block your ex for your own peace of mind, have at it. But if you can, just refrain from visiting his pages. I've been guilty of this. Once upon a time, I Insta-stalked one ex of mine every few days. And then he started posting about another woman, saying the same things about her that he had said about me. It became increasingly bad for my mental health, so I stopped online stalking him cold. Daily checking his social media pages did nothing good for me and kept me mired up in the past instead of moving on into my bright and amazing future. Remember, they are your ex for a reason. When you're tempted to sneak a peek at their Facebook

page, remember that reason. Then text or call a friend instead.

10. And, finally, take care of *you*. A breakup is hard, and it takes a toll on your mental, emotional, and even physical health. Make sure you're eating good foods, getting plenty of sleep, drinking water, exercising, spending time with friends, and doing other things you love. The beautiful thing about a breakup is that it teaches you what you want, don't want, and won't ever settle for again . . . so this can be a time of immense growth and change and positive momentum if you'll let it. Use all your newfound free time as an opportunity to reconnect with *you* and the things you love to do. Your work. Your hobbies. Your friends. Your breakup can be your glow-up, with the right attitude.

At the end of the day, breakups suck. There is nothing about them that is fun. But you don't have to lose yourself or even lose the lesson just because you lost the love. Breakups can be master classes in letting go, moving on, and coming out better and stronger on the other side. After all, sometimes it takes a heartbreak to shake us awake and help us see that we are worth so much more than we were settling for. A great way to move on from a breakup is to put all that time and energy you were putting into them into loving yourself. Moving on and living a fabulous life is the best revenge! When it comes down to it, the best way to move on is to remember that anyone who leaves your life does so because they are no longer meant to be there. So take a deep breath, open your hands and your heart, and let go. The life and love you deserve are waiting on the other side.

RULE TO Re-meme-ber

It's kind of funny . . . the things guys think we don't know.

Like when they fall off. Stop texting as much. Stop calling as much. Slowly begin to pull back. Even if it's ever so slowly . . . a little at a time. We know. Even if we don't want to admit it to ourselves, we know what it means.

It can be even a slight withdrawal of time and attention, and we feel it. Nothing gets by us women. We've been around this block a few times before. We know that he's not just having a busy day. We know that he didn't leave his phone at home. We know it's not simply that he has his mind on other things. We *know*.

We know there's someone else now on the receiving end of those texts and calls. We know his time and attention are going somewhere, just not to us. We know when we're being juggled. We know when we're being ghosted. We know when the energy shifts from us to someone else, no matter how subtly. We know when he's lost interest. We *know*.

It's kind of funny . . . the things guys think we don't know.

We know. We always know. And we might let him slide out of our DMs as easily as he slid in. We might look the other way or let it go or choose not to let him know that we know.

We might even let him off the hook for choosing to disappear instead of just telling us he was going.

But we know. Trust that.

We're women. Nothing gets by us.

Especially a man on his way out the door.

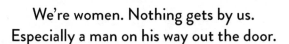

We're women. Nothing gets by us.
Especially a man on his way out the door.

26

He Loves Him, He Loves Me Not

Life after Loving a Narcissist

For a significant period of my life, I was in love with a narcissist.

Narcissists are adept at cultivating that protective instinct in the people they entangle themselves with . . . often so much so, you're willing to protect them no matter the cost to yourself.

What is a narcissist? Here are some character traits, according to BPDCentral.com:

- Lacks empathy: is unwilling to recognize or identify with the feelings and needs of others
- Has a grandiose sense of self-importance (e.g., exaggerates achievements and talents, expects to be recognized as superior without commensurate achievements)

- Has a sense of entitlement, i.e., unreasonable expectations of especially favorable treatment or automatic compliance with his or her expectations
- Is interpersonally exploitative, i.e., takes advantage of others to achieve his or her own ends
- Is often envious of others or believes others are envious of him or her
- Requires excessive admiration
- Shows arrogant, haughty behaviors or attitudes
- Believes that he or she is "special" and unique and can only be understood by, or should associate with, other special or high-status people (or institutions)
- Is preoccupied with fantasies of unlimited success, power, brilliance, beauty, or ideal love

You might have read about my ex Mr. E (aka "John") at some point along the way. If you are at all familiar with my work, you definitely have. I have written extensively about him in my books and on my blog. I've romanticized the relationship a lot. Not because I was trying to be dishonest in any way but because I was remembering the relationship as how I wanted it to be and remembering him as who I always hoped he would be instead of remembering things the way they really were. But that's another thing narcissists are great at: the grand yet empty gesture. They do something that's seemingly so big and flashy and grandiose that you fail to see how it's essentially a smoke screen, a bait and switch. The biggest example of this from my relationship with John is the mortifying episode we've already touched on when he shut down a jewelry store in Manhattan to show me engagement rings, only to then fail to propose. For every grand gesture, there was always an equally empty and meaningless reality hiding behind it. When I traveled to Las Vegas on my book tour several years ago and met up with him (as he was living there at the time), he showed up at my event wearing a hat that he had made that read "Mr. E" (the name I dubbed him in three of my four books to protect the not so innocent). He threw out some big talk about us going to a wedding chapel and getting married while I was in town. He made a big production out of our every moment together . . . and it felt big and exciting and romantic. Until I realized that he wanted more to be a character in my books than a presence in my life. He was a whole lot of glitter and very little gold—as most narcissists are.

After the tour, we officially became a couple. Or so I thought. Being in a long-distance relationship with someone who lacked the slightest ability to be emotionally open and supportive was one of the emptiest and most soul-sucking experiences of my entire life. He would talk about what an amazing boyfriend he was going to be and tell me how I was going to see a side of him I had never seen before . . . only to follow through with not a single one of his grand promises. I sent him letters and cards and little gifts in the mail, suggested we schedule Skype dates, and tried to encourage frequent and meaningful communication since we didn't get to spend time together face-to-face. He never sent me one thing in the mail, he made excuse after excuse about why he couldn't do a Skype date, and he would drop all communication for days at a time. He would just vanish, without explanation . . . one time for as long as a week . . . only to pop up again without remorse, apologies, or explanations. This all came to a head when he told me he had written me a long letter, detailing exactly how he felt about me. Considering that he had never given me a card in the entire time I had known him (Hello! Red flag alert! If you've been romantically involved with a man for years and have never seen his handwriting, that might be a sign that he's not the one for you.), I was obviously thrilled. Every day for a week, I ran to the mailbox, eagerly awaiting his letter.

And every day for a week, I returned to my apartment disappointed, internalizing his selfishness and his narcissism and interpreting it as something wrong with me: *I'm not worthy enough, I'm not attractive enough, I'm not lovable enough to warrant his time and attention.*

The letter episode kicked off a month of no contact. A *month*, y'all. We were in a relationship and I didn't know where my boyfriend was. If it wasn't so tragic, it would be comical. My calls and texts went unanswered until I finally gave up and withdrew from him completely. Withdrew into a painful shell. Allowed my heart to become hardened and guarded. Surrendered all the ideas and excitement and plans and dreams and hopes I had for the relationship. Some things really shut down in me during that time: a purity, an idealism, a belief in love that I had always held. It makes me sad to look back on that time and realize that every bit of the rejection, self-doubt, and pain I experienced was at the hand of someone who was supposed to love me. (By the way, he would tell me later that he "lost the letter." Who knows if it ever really even existed.)

Ultimately, our saga would drag on for three more years before he broke my heart one final time. And for a long time, I wasn't the same person I was before him. I wasn't as open, as trusting, as optimistic about my romantic future and my dreams of marriage and family. Over the past few years, and especially since I turned forty, I'm happy to say that I've started to find that part of myself again. I'm so relieved to know she's still in there. With time and counseling and prayer and healing, she has risen up from the ashes and begun to sparkle and believe and dream and dance and wish again, as she once did.

With time and distance, I've realized only in hindsight that the man I loved and trusted and believed in and supported and would have done anything for was not, in fact, the Prince Charming my heart and imagination wanted him to be. He was instead a narcissist who never had any significant attachment to me or intent to fulfill the love he had awakened in me. And I feel like it's time to get real, with both myself and with all of you, about the true story behind the romantic fairy tale I've spun in previous books in the hopes that I can help someone else who might be going through the motions with a narcissist and praying he will change.

Here's the thing: he won't. He's completely and totally incapable of it. He won't see the error of his ways because, in his mind, nothing is his fault. He won't apologize because, in his mind, he's done nothing wrong. And he won't ever love you like you deserve to be loved . . . because he's virtually incapable of loving anyone but himself. And besides, everything—and I mean *everything*—is about him. Your needs? Your boundaries? Your hopes and plans and fears and dreams and wishes? Completely inconsequential to him. And he'll gaslight you to the point that they will become inconsequential to you too . . . if you stick around long enough to let him.

And here's the part that's hard for me to say and even harder for you to hear (I know this because it was hard for me to accept about myself for a very long time). If you are consistently drawn to people (narcissists) who don't or can't love you well or right or enough, here's a secret: it's typically because *you* don't love *you* enough.

It might sound harsh, but I can say this with complete confidence as someone who didn't use to love myself, didn't use to show up for myself, didn't use to see my own worth, and did use to believe that the swipe defined my life: *it starts with you.* How you feel about yourself and how you treat yourself is how you will invite and allow other people to feel about and treat you. I accepted his narcissistic ways and poor treatment for years because I didn't believe I deserved anything better. And yes, sometimes people are just bad people and treat everyone around them badly, and it doesn't matter how much you love yourself, they're never going to love you (and usually the root cause of their "bad" is that they don't love themselves properly either). But, all that said, if this is a recurring pattern in your life and you keep attracting the same type of narcissistic people over and over and over, or you keep allowing the same narcissistic person to emotionally and/or mentally abuse you, there's something broken inside *you* that must be fixed before you can hope to attract or even desire a healthy, healed partner. Because when you love yourself—truly love yourself—you'll start choosing good men instead of bad boys or narcissistic boys or neglectful boys or emotionally abusive boys. It's just the facts.

If you recognize anything about yourself or your relationship in anything I've just said, walk away now. Don't wait another day or hour or second. Walk away and do not look back. Don't let an empty shell of a narcissistic person turn you into one too. Don't waste years of your life like I did. Walk away knowing you're not losing anything. You're actually gaining back your life, your sanity, your*self*.

Walk away from him and straight to a therapist's office . . . someone who can help you heal from what you've just been through and help you determine exactly why you chose to love someone who was so emotionally unavailable and unhealthy in the first place.

Sometimes I wish I could go back in time and avoid this whole experience. But then I think that perhaps by sharing my story with you, I might be able to save someone else from years of heartache. And that makes it all worth it to me.

RULE TO Re-meme-ber

It's not your fault that they don't know how to act . . .

But it *is* on you if you keep sticking around anyway.

Once is a mistake. Two or more times is a choice.

And if they keep choosing to hurt you, lie to you, betray you, disappoint you, abandon you . . .

Why do you keep choosing to stay?

If he's making you cry,

If he's making you question everything about yourself,
If he's gaslighting you,
If he's making you feel crazy,
If he's calling you crazy,
If he's turning you into a private detective trying to figure out what he's doing, feeling, and not feeling,
If he's constantly ignoring your needs in favor of his own,
And he's convincing you to do the same,
If being with him is in ANY way causing you to sacrifice your peace, your mental health, your friends, your confidence, your happiness, your family, your faith, your dignity, your self-esteem, your self-worth, your well-being, or yourself . . .
HE IS NOT THE ONE FOR YOU.
And if you lost him but found

- your peace of mind
- your happiness
- your dignity
- your confidence
- your smile
- your sanity
- yourself . . .

YOU WON.

If being with him is in ANY way causing you to sacrifice your peace, your mental health, your friends, your confidence, your happiness, your family, your faith, your dignity, your self-esteem, your self-worth, your well-being, or yourself . . .
HE IS NOT THE ONE FOR YOU.

27

Lose the Love, Keep the Lesson

Ten Things You Can Only Learn by Having Your Heart Broken

I've dealt with a lot of heartbreak in my time. Like . . . a *lot*. A few such instances I've talked about in this book. John. Chandler Bing. Johnny Castle. I take that back. That wasn't heart*break* I felt with Johnny Castle; it was heart*burn*. Ha!

But you know what? I had one really, really big heartbreak a few years ago—one of the top three biggest of my life—that I haven't talked about much publicly. I think we have to reserve the right to keep some things only for ourselves. In a world of oversharing, where our lives are skywritten daily across social media, it's important to keep some things sacred and only between us and God.

Instead of sharing the story of what happened and how it happened and why it happened . . . I thought I would share the lessons I learned *after* it happened. Just today I heard "I Will Always

Love You" by Whitney Houston on the radio, and even though it brought a tear to my eye, I know that my present—and future—is infinitely better and calmer and healthier without this relationship.

The season following a breakup is such a vulnerable one. If you're not careful, you can get caught up in letting the swipe rule your life by dwelling on the negative instead of focusing on the positive and what can be learned from the relationship that will make you better and stronger in future relationships. The negative, of course, being the rejection. The fear that this might have been your last chance at love (spoiler alert: there's no such thing as a "last chance at love" as long as you are alive and breathing). The anxiety that comes with losing someone who has been a huge part of your life for a significant amount of time. The emptiness that suddenly looms in your life now that your normal routine with your partner has been completely disrupted. And so on and so forth.

I want to encourage you to lean into that vulnerability and look a little closer, because behind every big emotion that comes along with a big loss is an even bigger lesson. I'm not saying you have to go out for a skip on the sunny side of the street five minutes after heartbreak has run you over like a semitruck. I'm simply suggesting you remain open to the idea that this person who just left you or who you just left might have been the *wrong* one . . . but that doesn't mean they can't teach you something that will help prepare you for the *right* one. Just because you lost the love doesn't mean you have to lose the lesson.

So, without further ado, I bring you . . . the top ten things you can only learn by having your heart broken. For those of you who are haunted by ghosts from the past, perhaps this will give you the courage and the gumption to put them to rest and move on, once and for all. Because, while they might have left you and taken their Hulu account with them, they didn't leave you empty-handed.

1. First impressions are everything. Those little red flags (or giant red flags) you see waving ever so subtly in the

breeze on day one will be massive stop signs by day one hundred, I promise you. My ex lied to me pretty early into our relationship about something fairly significant, and it started us off on the entirely wrong foot. I wanted to give him the benefit of the doubt and try to get past the lie. So I did . . . but it continued to haunt the relationship and played a huge part in its demise. Had I taken that red flag of dishonesty at face value the moment it happened, I would have saved myself months of pain and heartache.

2. How they are in life = how they are in love. My ex was generally a decent guy at heart, but his life was very . . . chaotic. He had financial struggles and work struggles and his house was constantly a wreck and he just couldn't seem to get it together. Obviously, no one is perfect, and I loved him right there in the middle of his mess . . . but eventually the chaos that swirled around him took over my life as well. It took me months to get my life back together after the hurricane that was our relationship stormed through.
3. Chemistry does not and should not outweigh compatibility. My ex and I had it going on in the chemistry department, so much so that I think I fell in love with him a little bit when he kissed me on our first date. But that instant connection we shared acted as smoke and mirrors to the reality of the person behind the kiss. Chemistry can take you only so far . . . but it's much like someone handing you a beautifully wrapped box that's empty. It doesn't matter how good and attractive and appealing the exterior looks if what's beneath the surface is disappointing or lacking.
4. When you ask God with complete and total sincerity to remove anyone from your life who doesn't belong there,

be prepared for Him to do it. As our relationship started to deteriorate more and more, I clung for dear life to what I knew was a sinking ship. I was terrified to surrender the situation to God because I knew the minute I did, He would take it away. And I wasn't ready to give it up. Until I was. One night I worked up my nerve and finally said the hard prayer and surrendered and asked God to remove the relationship from my life if it wasn't in His will for me. The next day, my ex broke up with me. As painful as it was, I had the peace of knowing God wouldn't have taken it so swiftly and abruptly had the relationship been meant for me.

5. You can fight to the death for a relationship, but if you're the only one fighting, it's a losing battle. I wanted with all my heart for that relationship to work, but just one person showing up to battle every day will never be enough. Eventually you will buckle under the emotional weight of fighting all alone. And should love be a constant battle anyway? It was never going to work, no matter how hard I fought, because he was the wrong person for me, and I was the wrong person for him. You can be the right person all day long, but if you're with the wrong person . . . nothing you do will save the relationship. I'm grateful for the experience though. It taught me about the kind of person I want to be in relationships and showed me how far I still needed to go to get there. I realized that I had to learn to fight for myself as hard as I had been fighting for that relationship. And that realization has changed my life.
6. If someone loves you, *really* loves you, they will love all of you. The good and the bad, the dark and the light, the beautiful and the ugly. There is no part of you they will run from. They will stay and fight, with you and for you. When my anxiety started to (understandably) show up

in our relationship due to the early episode of dishonesty, it all just became too much of a hurdle to overcome. The thing is, love isn't blind. Nor should it be. If love was blind, would it really be love? Love sees your flaws and inadequacies and imperfections and anxieties and loves you anyway. And love never, ever uses those things against you or cites them as reasons not to be with you. Love is too busy loving the stuffing out of you to even pause to dwell on the flaws. Love recognizes that we are all a little banged up and broken and bruised by the rolls and punches of life and that does not make us unlovable. In fact, I daresay the fact that we are all those things yet still believe in love makes us all the more lovable.

7. A person who really, truly loves you will always show up for you. They will meet you halfway. Sometimes even more than halfway. Love, as the Bible says, covers a multitude of sins. It doesn't hesitate or doubt or pause on the shore . . . it jumps in to meet you right where you are. And then it hangs on through the wind and waves and turbulence and refuses to let go just because things get a little uncertain or stormy or shaky. Love will be the first one in the door and the last one out. *Love shows up.* Love perseveres. Love is all in. Always.
8. You can tell a lot more about a person's character by how they end a relationship than by how they begin one. My relationship ended in a five-minute phone call. Five minutes and my heart was broken. It took about a year for me to fully recover . . . and then another year to find out that my gut was right all along . . . that he wasn't right for me. How they leave your life is a lot more telling about the kind of person they are than how they arrive. And though it might be painful and heartbreaking and so hard to accept . . . who they are in those last five minutes

. . . is who they are. And if they weren't kind and gentle and mindful with your heart in those last five minutes, they never would have been a good steward of it in the long run.

9. When it's over, it's over. Let it be over. Stop trying to resurrect it. Stop arguing with God about why you should still have it. Stop worrying about what went wrong or torturing yourself about what you could have done differently or better. There is nothing you could have done differently or better. You can't turn the wrong one into the right one, no matter how hard you try. Take a deep breath and let go. Cry. Grieve. Give yourself time and space to feel the loss. Acceptance and grace are key here. Allowing yourself to mourn the end is key here. The relationship mattered. Your feelings for the other person were real and they mattered. Your heartbreak is real and it matters. But it's still over. Let it go. And when you're ready . . . really ready . . . try again with someone new. Don't allow the loss of one relationship or one broken heart stop you from trying again. Always be willing to try again. Love is worth the risk.
10. You are stronger than you think you are. You can and will survive the end of this relationship. And you won't just survive . . . you will *thrive*. You will someday, not too long from now, be stronger and wiser and better for having loved this person *and* for having lost him (even if you can't see it right now).

RULE TO Re-meme-ber

Sometimes power is staying and fighting for what, and whom, you love . . . and sometimes power is realizing that it's time to stop fighting a losing battle and walk away from the battlefield with dignity and grace.

Sometimes power doesn't feel like power in the moment.

Sometimes it feels like heartbreak.

Sometimes it feels like defeat.

Sometimes it feels like the loss of everything that matters.

Settling for someone who's not meant for you out of fear that no one else will come along is easy.

Refusing to settle for anything less than the best and walking away is hard.

But an unwillingness to settle is what separates the women from the girls.

Loving yourself too much to stick around where you're not loved enough or loved well is a mark of strength. And losing the love but refusing to lose the lesson? Well, that's just downright superhero status.

So even though right now you hurt and ache and can't see past your heartbreak . . . someday you'll thank God that the person you thought you wanted so bad, turned out to be the best thing you never had.

Sometimes power is staying and fighting for what, and whom, you love . . . and sometimes power is realizing that it's time to stop fighting a losing battle and walk away from the battlefield with dignity and grace.

28

Taking Back Your Territory

Why Ex Doesn't Get to Mark the Spot

Over the past three or four years, I've dated exactly six guys. When I say "dated," I mean a relationship that went beyond a handful of dates and turned into something more substantial. Only one of them was super serious, and another was somewhat serious (the on/off situation with John that lasted over a decade and was always too on to be casual and too off to be serious). But even though only two of the relationships were serious or fairly serious, all of them left their mark emotionally, on me and my heart, and physically, on my surroundings. By that I mean we spent time together in my apartment, we spent time together in my small town, we spent time together in the places that surround me every single day. And as a sentimental person, I get attached not just to people but to locations, places that were significant to a relationship and the memories we made there. It can be hard once a relationship ends to feel comfortable going back to places I once went with that person I cared about. And that can make it tricky to walk through my everyday life without hearing an Adele song (literally any one of them) on a loop in my mind *all the time*.

For example, one of my exes and I had our first kiss just about three blocks from my apartment. Which was all fine and good and beautiful and romantic while we were together, but once we broke up (painfully), it was nearly impossible for me to go within a block of that location without feeling sick to my stomach. And that was extremely problematic for me because I love my neighborhood. I take walks around my neighborhood all the time. I go to the farmers market on summer weekends. I attend the Christmas tree lighting in the winter. To have a great big emotional black hole that I felt I had to avoid like the plague just wasn't going to work for me.

So, one day, a few months after we broke up and a few months after I had grown weary of dodging that area of my neighborhood, I decided enough was enough. The relationship had ended—and not just ended but ended abruptly in a five-minute-long phone call like it never really mattered to him at all. So why was I still allowing that relationship and that person to dictate my movements and my feelings about an area of town that I loved? Why was I letting the swipe rule my life? It had to stop.

I took a deep breath, worked up all the nerve I had, and walked right down that sidewalk where that first kiss with my ex had happened all those months ago. Right down the center of it. I didn't waver or dodge or hesitate. I was done with all that. I was done letting someone else control my life. *I reclaimed that spot.* And you know what? I expected to feel a rush of emotions and sadness and nostalgia, but I really didn't. All I felt was pride and strength and deep gratitude that I was no longer stuck in the intense cloud of grief that had descended upon my life when the relationship ended. I was not the same person I had been just a few months prior. I was stronger, wiser, and braver. And right then and there on a beautiful summer day, I Marie Kondo'd that ex right out of my heart and off my town square. He no longer sparked joy for me, but that didn't mean my beloved town square still couldn't. I took it back! And it felt amazing.

Sometimes that's just what we have to do. We have to reclaim locations, memories . . . parts of ourselves . . . that we lost to failed relationships and heartbreak. When the dust settles from the end of a relationship, it can sometimes feel like we've lost absolutely everything. Places and spaces and familiar faces suddenly seem rife with the fear of having to relive every laugh—and, yes, every tear—each time we cross the threshold of somewhere we once tread with our ex. But it doesn't have to be that way. We don't have to surrender these great big pieces of our hearts and our lives to people who didn't love us enough to stick around. We don't have to lose ourselves just because we lost the love. We can reclaim not just significant places but also our time and our happiness just by simply refusing to allow the memory of someone who isn't even in our lives anymore to control us.

I have a girlfriend who, when she broke up with her boyfriend, went around with a new friend to every restaurant and every significant location where she and her ex had been to make new memories. She didn't dodge or avoid or shy away from those painful chapters with her ex; she simply rewrote the story. She refused to believe the swipe and instead took back her life! And that is what we must do when someone walks away from us and we're still surrounded by their memory. We must decide to release the emotional and physical ties we have to them the same way they released us. It's the only way to be free.

When a relationship ends, we tend to want to seek closure, sometimes to our own detriment. But nothing the other person could say or do will ever really serve as a satisfactory period on the end of the sentence that was your relationship. It's still going to hurt and it's still going to be hard and you're still going to have questions. Things are still going to feel unfinished because that's what a relationship that ends is: unfinished. I used to think that closure was something I had to wait for someone else to give me. Then one day my therapist told me that closure is up to me and me alone and that I was giving away my power by looking to someone else to give me what I should be giving myself. The truth is . . . closure happened the minute they chose to walk away. It doesn't really matter why they walked away. The ending is still the same.

The beautiful thing about reclaiming your territory and places that are significant to you is that it gives you the chance to create your own closure. It allows you to release the weight of those memories of past relationships in a very positive and even visceral way. To wipe the slate clean. To stop torturing yourself with the thought of what might have been and instead look ahead to what can still be. You don't have to do anything fancy to reclaim your spaces and take back your power. Even if you just go stand in the location and whisper to yourself, "I reclaim this space!" that's all it takes. It can be your way of adding that period to the end of the sentence and closing that chapter once and for all . . . instead of waiting for someone to close it for you.

I urge you to reclaim your power by releasing the dead weight of whatever little pieces of past relationships you're still holding on to: maybe a ring or another significant item, or maybe the emotional weight of avoiding places you once loved because they remind you of someone you once loved. Whatever you may be holding on to—silently thank these things for the role they played in your life and the lessons they taught you. Then let them all go and take back your happiness. Make new memories. Reclaim your territory *and* your life. Because there's still lots of treasure to be found on the road ahead . . . and ex doesn't mark the spot.

RULE TO Re-meme-ber

Sometimes closure arrives two years later, on an ordinary Friday afternoon, in a way you never expected or could have predicted. Sometimes it comes while standing on a street corner where you once had your first kiss with a guy you would go on to love and then lose.

And you cry a little and you laugh a little, and for the first time in a long time . . . you exhale. You are *free*.

That's the thing about closure. It can arrive on any day, at any time. Sometimes it's weeks, sometimes months, sometimes even years later. Sometimes other people give it to you. But most of the time, closure is a gift you give yourself. You can rarely know when or how it will come. And you can't wait around or put your life on hold looking for it.

But given enough time . . .

Closure always comes.

And it feels like freedom.

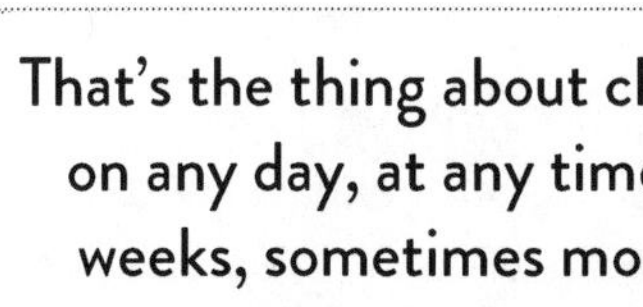

That's the thing about closure. It can arrive on any day, at any time. Sometimes it's weeks, sometimes months, sometimes even years later. Sometimes other people give it to you. But most of the time, closure is a gift you give yourself.

29

You Are the Sun

How to Find Love without Losing Yourself

Wow, we've taken quite a journey together.

We've dated. We've online dated. We've been out on good dates and bad dates. We've been ghosted. We've been zombied. We've been kissed badly. We've been kissed well. We've been kissed goodbye. We've kissed dating goodbye. We've been glamboozled (I had to work that word into the book before we got to the end . . . ha!). We've learned the difference between a textationship, a situationship, and a relationship. We've learned to stop apologizing for believing that we are worthy of the very best love has to offer. We've talked allllll things exes . . . and we've determined that we're completely here for rain boots and cowboy boots and even Ugg boots, but never *re*boots. We've dug deep to identify ways we were losing ourselves to the dating process. We've come to realize that it's okay to take breaks from dating altogether. We've identified the distinction between *boo* and *bae* (and that there's really not one). We've survived a few breakups and regretted a few makeups. We've learned how to let go: of the need to control, of the need to always know, and of toxic mindsets, relationship patterns, and people. We've learned how to stop waiting around on any man to love us and instead love ourselves. We've learned that Jerry Maguire was in fact just a movie, and it's no one's responsibility to "complete" us except our own. We've taken back our power and reclaimed our territory and stopped making excuses for halfhearted men and declared that, no, we would not like fries with that, because we are no one's side item.

We've explored all the ways we were believing the swipe and defeating ourselves . . .

And we've given ourselves permission to say, "to the left, to the left"—to all of it.

And now here we are, almost at the end of our journey. But before we say #thankunext to our time together, I want to impart something to you that my therapist shared with me a couple of years ago. Something that was so mind and life altering, it was worth every penny I've ever spent in therapy, just to hear this one sentence.

(*Wait for it . . .*)

I'm a *big* believer in therapy, as you've probably clued in to by now. I think everyone should be in therapy. We are all constantly growing and changing and struggling and overcoming. And let's face it—life is just plain hard at times. Especially for a single woman out here volunteering as tribute in *The Hunger Games* that is modern dating. We all need someone to talk to, and we all have things we could use an unbiased person to help us work on. Some of my biggest struggles, as I've shared with you throughout this book, have been maintaining my identity in relationships, not allowing the swipe to define my life, and learning how to search for love without losing myself. To be honest, I've struggled with losing myself in relationships of really any kind, romantic ones *and* friendships. I struggle to find balance between my personal life and my professional life, and I can be guilty of becoming single-minded. For example, I'll go through phases where I morph into such a social butterfly that I let my work completely slip. Or I'll get so caught up in the guy I'm dating that I lose touch with my friends. Or I'll get so wrapped up in my work that I allow it to eclipse everything else.

Where does this lack of balance and lifelong battle to not lose myself in someone else stem from? Well, for one thing, I'm human. I think humans in general struggle with balance in their lives. But in my case (and I suspect this is true for a lot of people), it's also because, in the past, I was guilty of attributing my worth to other people. How other people treated me or responded to me or loved me or didn't love me tended to be the playbook I followed for determining how I was going to treat myself or love myself. That's why I would often get so wrapped up in other people and in earning their approval or time or love or attention that I would completely lose track of myself. And that, my friends, is a recipe for unhappiness. Why? Because it's all backwards. *You* have to determine your worth, and then other people will fall in line with your beliefs. If you wait around on other people to decide how you're going to feel about yourself, you will always be miserable, unhappy, and unfulfilled. If you wait around on other people to "complete" you . . . you will always be unfinished.

Or, as my therapist put so succinctly a couple of years ago . . .

(*Here it comes . . .*)

"You are the sun in your solar system. Everyone else in your life rotates around you. You do not rotate around them."

Good grief, did you just hear all the mics in the land drop after that, or is it just me?! That's a #truthbomb, #yassssqueen, #thatpart all rolled into one! It reminds me of one of my all-time favorite *Grey's Anatomy* quotes, said by Cristina to Meredith about McDreamy:

"Don't let what *he* wants eclipse what *you* need. He's very dreamy, but he's not the sun. You are."

How many of you, like me, have surrendered your sunlight to stand in someone else's shade? In one of my more serious relationships, we fell in love very quickly and things moved at warp speed, so much so that a couple of months into the relationship, we were already talking marriage. I was so excited to find this great love that I completely—and I mean *completely*—surrendered myself and my life over to the relationship. Which sounds really lovely and romantic in theory but, in reality, spells disaster for a relationship. Why? Because when the other person met you, they fell for the you that had a life other than them. And when that busy, vibrant, full life gets pushed to the side in order to make the relationship the center of your universe, everything gets thrown off balance. In my case, when we met, I was busy writing and spending lots of time with friends, and I had tons of other things going on other than that relationship. In other words, I was the sun. I was shining brilliantly. And that's who my ex fell for. But slowly, a little at a time, I made *him* the sun. And the more I made him the sun, the more I stopped shining. I went against my gut several times at key moments in our relationship, but I was scared to speak up for fear of hurting his feelings. The same thing happened again the first time he told me he loved me. I knew I was on my way to falling in love with him, but I wasn't quite there yet and wasn't ready to actually say the words. Yet I went against my gut and said it back because I didn't want to lose him (or in other words, I was completely, totally, 100 percent letting the swipe rule my life).

The more I rotated around him and the more I sacrificed my needs for his wants, the more our relationship deteriorated. You can guess what happened next. I was left alone in the darkness, having surrendered my shine to someone else.

Where did I go wrong? I made him the sun. I didn't maintain any sort of balance or set healthy boundaries in the relationship. And the relationship spun off its axis until there was no way to recover. I had found love, but I had lost myself in the process. And that's too big a price to pay for *any* relationship.

So how can you make sure you remain the sun in your relationships? Here are a few easy tips:

1. Maintain your life outside of your relationship. Don't be that girl who completely bails on her life, her friendships, and her hobbies for any man. You don't need to see him every night of the week. My ex and I would often sacrifice sleep to spend time together and wind up exhausted and miserable the next day. That inevitably leads to resentment and is not a healthy foundation for a relationship. Keep going to the gym, keep having girls' nights out, keep up with your self-care. A relationship is designed to add to your already awesome life . . . not completely eclipse it.
2. Set healthy boundaries and listen to your gut. Establish how many days you're going to see him in a week and don't apologize for it. If you're not ready to take a great big relationship step like meeting the kids or saying I love you . . . don't. You can't just agree to everything the other person asks of you because you're afraid you'll lose them if you disagree. Speak up and make your needs known. A relationship that isn't a two-way street is a dead-end road.
3. Finally, throw out the notion that you need anyone or anything to complete you. You are already a whole, complete person just as you are. Or as I like to say, you are the cake, and a relationship is the icing. With or without the icing, a cake is still a cake!

And here's the thing, you great big beautiful cake: even when you do all those things, sometimes the person you want more than anything still won't choose you. Or sometimes they'll choose you and then put you back. No matter how great a catch you are, you're going to sometimes get dropped. That's just the way this modern dating game goes. But we must still remain the sun, regardless of who spins in and out of our orbit.

We must respect ourselves.

We must value ourselves.

We must love ourselves.

Regardless of who chooses us or doesn't choose us, we must choose ourselves.

If life is a schoolyard pick . . . choose *you*. Be your own team. Be your own best friend. Be your own tribe. Be your own person. Be your own better half. Be your own number-one draft pick. Become so overflowing with self-love that the people who didn't choose you will wish they had. And the people who did . . . will know they didn't get just a girl, but the whole world.

You are *everything*. Stop waiting on people who are anything or nothing to validate that or confirm that or cosign that. You don't need their approval. You don't need their permission. You don't need their affirmation. You never did.

Stop waiting on them to choose you and choose yourself. You are deserving of all the love in the world, starting with your own. You deserve to be chosen. When you choose you, when you love you . . . it no longer matters a bit what anyone else is doing. Or not doing.

You, more than anybody in the world, are worthy of your own love.

Let them choose what they will.

You choose *you*.

Because until you view yourself as a choice . . . and treat yourself like a choice . . . you'll always be someone's option.

And until you view yourself as the sun and start behaving like the sun . . . you'll always be wildly and chaotically spinning around everyone else in your life rather than allowing them to rotate in and out of your life as *you* choose.

Choose you. Choose you. Always choose you. *You are your best thing.*

When you choose you, you won't care if they swipe left because you will have already swiped right on yourself.

RULE TO Re-meme-ber

The time to stop letting the swipe rule your life is *now*. The time to step into and own your worth is *now*. The time to stop settling for people and relationships that are unworthy of you is *now*. The time to stop accepting crumbs when you are worth the whole entire meal is *now*.

No more half-baked, indecisive, wishy-washy people. No more almost relationships or not-quite situationships. No more ghosters and flakes and love bombers and zombies and seekhers and kittenfishers and Houdinis. No more nonsense. *No more. No more. No more.*

Only YOU can decide that you are worth more than you've been settling for.

From here on out, we are loving ourselves the way we want to be loved. We are teaching people how to treat us. We are finding love without losing ourselves. We are jacking our standards to Jesus, and those who can't rise to our level are getting left in our dust. Unapologetically.

We are absolutely, unequivocally *done* believing the swipe. Who's with me?

Only YOU can decide that you are worth more than you've been settling for.

30

I'll Take That to Go

A Few à la Carte Rules for the Road

I had a few bonus Rules to Re-*meme*-ber left over that didn't quite fit into a particular chapter, so I collected them all here. And remember! The only rule in Swipe Club . . . is to talk about Swipe Club. To anyone and everyone you meet (wink wink).

I had a girl message me recently and ask me, "How do I tell this guy who keeps messaging me on Facebook that I'm not interested in him and I no longer wish to hear from him? I don't want to be mean." Friends, it is not mean to not be interested in someone! It is not mean to say, "Thanks, but no thanks." It is not mean to politely tell someone that you appreciate their interest, but you simply don't reciprocate it. It's not mean to not want someone to repeatedly message you and borderline badger you. *You don't owe anyone anything*, and you especially don't owe anyone feelings that you don't have. We must realize that we are allowed to say no. We are allowed to say "pass." We are allowed to swipe left. We are allowed to determine who and what stays in our lives and who and what goes. Without apologizing for it. Period. End of sentence.

Your standards are not too high, your boundaries are not too strong, your expectations of being treated well and with respect are not too unreasonable. You don't want too much and you're not asking for too much just because you want loyalty and ask for honesty. Anyone who makes you feel like you are too much is simply not enough for you. Don't lower your standards to accommodate those who refuse to raise theirs. If they can't meet you at your level, then perhaps they shouldn't get to meet you at all.

One thing I've learned, and I know this to be an absolute certainty: you should never have to wait around for someone to love you back. You should never have to wait around for someone to be "ready." You should never have to wait around for someone to love you the way you deserve to be loved. You should never have to wait around for someone to make their intentions and feelings clear. You should never have to wait around at all. True love is ready. True love is sure. True love is crystal clear. Anything else . . . isn't love.

Yes, you will have to work for the things you want, but you will never have to force the things you want. This is where people tend to get tripped up. Whether it's a relationship, a friendship, a dream job . . . whatever . . . if you're working your fingers to the bone for it and sweating and stressing and plotting and planning to make it yours, it is not for you. What is for you will flow toward you. What is not will flow away from you. Never resist the current. If it's not yours, you don't want it. Trust and let go.

Remember, if he says he's not enough for you . . . believe him. He's not enough for you. Don't waste your time trying to convince him otherwise or trying to lessen yourself to make him feel less inadequate. The right one for you will bask in your shine . . . he won't be intimidated by it or try to diminish it.

People are not Band-Aids. Relationships are not Band-Aids. You don't need another person to heal the damage that the last person did. You need self-care and therapy and time. Give yourself that time. Love when you're ready, not when you're lonely.

Ladies, here's the thing: if a man has to "consider" whether or not he wants to be with you . . . he doesn't want to be with you. Stop letting him waste your time, and move on with your life. You deserve someone who is so sure of you, they can't wait to make you theirs. Not someone who treats you like an option instead of making you his choice.

When they tell you they're not ready for a relationship . . . believe them.

When they tell you that you're not on the same page and you want different things . . . believe them.

When they tell you that you're "too much" for them . . . believe them.

When they say they never want to be married . . . believe them.

When they say all these things to you only to turn around and go get into a relationship with someone else . . . believe them.

When the only thing they're consistent in is their ability to disappoint you . . . believe them.

When someone shows you who they are . . . believe them.

Then let them go.

A moment will come, as it does in all relationships, where the love is one-sided or the effort is unbalanced, when you can either love him or love you . . . but you cannot continue to do both.

When that moment comes, it is vital that you choose correctly.

It is vital that you choose you, for all the times he didn't.

It is vital that you refuse to let go of yourself by clinging to someone else.

Yes, sometimes loving you means letting them go.

Let go. Let go. Let all the way go.

Because sometimes loving *you* means losing *him.*

It's a very freeing moment, the day you decide that you aren't going to let your relationship status define your life.

The day you decide that standing alone no longer intimidates you . . . it inspires you.

Being happy with others is great.

Being happy alone is greater.

Because it's real happiness, happiness that isn't based on anyone or anything, happiness that you cultivated for yourself, happiness that can never be taken from you.

It is only when you learn to stand alone in power that you're ready to stand together.

I once knew a girl who would send men scroll-length text messages when they broke up with her, detailing all the reasons she was over them and moving on with her life, and she thought this was empowering. Guess what? Chances are, those men either dismissed those texts or called the girl crazy to their friends. True empowerment is realizing that sometimes the best response is no response. A man who has made it clear he doesn't want to be with you is unworthy of any further communication from you. Period. The best, most empowered thing you can do is let a man who has made it clear he's moving on . . . go ahead and move on right outta your life. *And* your inbox. If he wants to experience life without you, let him! But never sacrifice your dignity trying to point out your worth to someone who doesn't care and isn't listening. Your worth is a fixed point and never needs to be argued or defended. Sometimes the most empowering thing you can say . . . is nothing at all.

Be grateful for those who stay.
But be just as grateful for those who leave.
Everyone who crosses your path serves a purpose.
If they are not a great love, they are surely a great lesson. And sometimes, they are both.

Girlfriend, if you haven't met his friends, if he hasn't met yours, if your "relationship" only exists in the dark, if he's all over your social media and there's no sign of you on his, if he keeps you hidden in any way, shape, or form, if he guards his phone like he's carrying around matters of national security on it, and if he keeps you playing a perpetual game of Where's Waldo? (games are cute as kids; not so much when you're grown) . . . he is not your boyfriend, so stop giving him boyfriend privileges. Never make someone your choice who is only keeping you around as an option.

You are magic.
And not everyone can handle magic.

Some people are so accustomed to mediocre that they run from magic.

Let them run.

Let them have their blah, their boring, their beige, their basic.

You just keep standing all tall and strong and sparkly in your magic, and let the ones who can't handle you pass you right on by.

Something about turning forty made all the pieces come together for me. I stopped leaving my self-worth in the hands of everyone around me and I took back my power. I stopped waiting on men to act right and started releasing relationships in which I was doing all the heavy lifting and finally, finally came to the realization that I am not just "enough" . . . I'm actually pretty awesome. And the most amazing thing happened. As my self-worth began to rise, so did my happiness. And my confidence. And my inner peace. I am finally okay with living in my skin and just being *me*. You don't have to wait until you're forty to get there. You can decide today that you're taking back your confidence and your self-worth. And you can start taking steps to do it. Take inventory of your life and figure out the relationships that are bringing you more hurt than happiness and let them go. Stop waiting on friends and love interests to join you in the things you want to do, and get out there and start living and having adventures, with or without someone by your side. This is your life, and you are your most beautiful constant. It's time to start loving and valuing yourself for always having your own back . . . right here, right now, in this moment. Because when your self-worth rises, your life follows.

And when you stop believing the swipe, you reclaim your life.

The End.

Acknowledgments

I'll keep this simple. Thank you from the bottom of my heart to my publishers at Revell and especially Vicki Crumpton for believing in me and in this book. Thanks also to my agent, Alexander Field; to my family, whom I adore more than anything in this world; and to my readers, who have stuck with me for over a decade now. This book, and every book I write, is for YOU.

Mandy Hale is a blogger turned *New York Times* bestselling author and speaker. Creator of the social media movement The Single Woman, Mandy cuts to the heart of single life with her inspirational, straight-talking, witty takes on life and love. Named a "Twitter Powerhouse" by the *Huffington Post*, a "Woman of Influence" by the *Nashville Business Journal*, one of the "Top-Ten Most Inspirational Instagram Accounts to Follow" by *Good Morning America*, and a "Single in the City" by *Nashville Lifestyles* magazine, she has also been featured in *Forbes* magazine, on Glamour.com, and many other media outlets. She is the author of *The Single Woman*; *I've Never Been to Vegas, but My Luggage Has*; *Beautiful Uncertainty*; and *You Are Enough*. She lives in Murfreesboro, Tennessee.